MACHINE
GUNS

MACHINE GUNS

Terry Gander

The Crowood Press

First published in 2003 by
The Crowood Press Ltd
Ramsbury, Marlborough
Wiltshire SN8 2HR

www.crowood.com

British Library Cataloguing-in-Publication Data
A catalogue record for this book is available from the British Library.

ISBN 1 86126 580 8

Typeset by Florence Production Ltd, Stoodleigh, Devon EX16 9PN

Contents

Introduction

Without setting out to do so, the designers, engineers and technicians who developed the early machine guns managed to devise the prototypes of an end product that helped to define the social course of the twentieth century. What commenced as a technical approach towards delivering fully automatic infantry small arms fire resulted in a weapon group that came to dominate battlefields from the first decade of the last century onwards, culminating in the mechanized slaughter of the 1914–18 Great War. During that conflict, the machine gun, along with artillery, was responsible for the deaths of so many of the finest young men that the combatant nations could produce, that the subsequent diverse political and social paths followed after 1918 could never revert to their former seemingly established structures. The result, far from the battlefield, was social upheaval on a massive scale, yet more conflict and, ultimately, the worst World War endured to date, all followed by the unsettling threat of nuclear warfare.

Of course, not all the events of the twentieth century were dictated by the machine gun, but a significant proportion of them most certainly were. From the Russo-Japanese War of 1904–05 onwards, the machine gun dominated the battlefield, at that time the only apparent theatre for settling international squabbles. As a result, infantry tactics and all other aspects of modern warfare, from the factories to the front lines, had to alter accordingly. The former autocratic chain of command, extending from on high and passing down to the lower echelons, could no longer operate in a world increasingly dominated by industrial technology and the ever-increasing pace of events, both on the battlefield and in the home-based factories and fields that fed the conflict. Authority had to devolve at a rate accelerated by the ever-widening scope of the Great War, to the extent that within a few years the old autocratic orders had been swept aside.

The uncontrollable devolution of authority away from centralized executive structures meant that decision-making reached levels of people who had never been previously trained or indoctrinated to assume and exercise authority – but such challenges were assumed with alacrity. Soldiers, and civilians, formerly conditioned to simply obeying orders without question while accepting the status quo, discovered that they could develop their own initiatives and put them into practice. In a phrase, people discovered they could determine their own futures.

The old monolithic orders were from then onwards doomed to fade away to be replaced by new and all too often unpredictable social structures, often with unfortunate long-term results. Numerous attempts were made to re-impose the old ways, most such policies eventually leading to yet more conflict, both internal and external, as populations exercised their uncertain and untested self-determinations. The course of the twentieth century became established not by autocracies but by social unrest. That state of affairs continues into the twenty-first century, with the machine gun still playing a lethally active part in proceedings.

* * *

For the purposes of this account, only machine guns with calibres of up to 15mm/0.59in will be considered. Above that calibre automatic weapons are termed as cannon, an area of study worthy of its own narrative. Also not included are sub-machine guns, which may be differentiated from machine guns by their pistol cartridges, with all their limitations in range and other factors.

Below 15mm/0.59in there have been numerous makes, types and models of machine gun. To list them all would take far more pages than are available here, but even so a few oddities and rarely mentioned weapons have been included. All the main and most important models are covered and it should be noted that new models seem to appear all the time, although it has to be commented that recent years have witnessed few new arrivals.

Again, for the purposes of this account, dimensions and/or weights used to denote or designate any particular weapon at the time it entered service will be employed. This avoids numerous references such as 0.303in/7.7mm and the approach will, hopefully, provide a more historical setting for the items described.

1 Beginnings

FIREPOWER

Out the outset, it should be explained why there was (and still is) a need for automatic-fire weapons. It all boils down to one military fundamental, namely firepower. From the time of simply hurling rocks at an opponent, it rapidly became apparent that the more missiles were being delivered at any one time, the greater the chances of inflicting harm to that opponent. The opponent either had to endure injury, seek protection behind cover, or take recourse to flight.

Archery advanced the firepower concept over the javelins and similar hurled weapons that preceded the introduction of longbows and cross-bows, massed longbows in particular demonstrating how firepower could inflict considerable damage to the opposition. The advent of black powder and the resultant early firearms simply added to the firepower potential, a potential that was not to be fully realized for many years as the technology was not there to produce anything other than slow-firing, single-shot weapons such as the musket. For many decades, the bow and the musket co-existed side by side.

The smooth bore musket was a clumsy, inaccurate weapon, but it was demonstrably superior to the longbow, with that weapon's limited and uncertain wounding power in other than highly practised hands, especially against an armoured adversary. The capabilities of the musket ball eventually rendered body armour obsolete. However, combat ranges remained short; the chances of an individual musket user hitting an opponent were uncertain other than at very close ranges, typically below 50m, and even then the only sure method of inflicting significant damage to the opposition was by synchronized volley fire. That entailed rigid drills to make sure all muskets were fired together at the correct instant, thereby creating maximum damage by partially overcoming the inaccuracy factor and amplifying the shock effect. British infantry, in particular, came to excel in controlled volley fire, even after the musket's replacement, the rifle, came into vogue at the beginning of the nineteenth century.

By adding spiral rifling grooves along the interior of the barrel, not only could a projectile be rendered more stable during its trajectory, and thus more accurate, but it could carry its casualty-inflicting kinetic energy to a greater range. This quality had been recognized by the end of the Napoleonic Wars, yet the widely distributed muskets (and their drills) were retained for several more decades. The early muzzle-loaded rifles required both time and practised skill to reload efficiently under battlefield conditions. They were more difficult to manufacture and so were more expensive than smooth-bore muskets.

At the beginning of the American Civil War in 1861, the infantry of both sides was still being issued with muskets as well as more modern rifles. By the end of that war in 1865, the rifle was ascendant, having inflicted dreadful casualties at long ranges during battles such as Cold Harbor and Gettysburg. From then on, the rifle became a universal issue for all European armies, its advantages being enhanced by the gradual adoption of the more powerful smokeless propellants from about 1866 onwards. Apart from avoiding the dense smoke clouds produced when igniting black powder, the improved power of the new propellants could launch a projectile much further and with enhanced muzzle energy. Large calibre bullets were thus no longer necessary. Smaller, elongated bullets fired at high velocity could deliver far more striking power and a soldier could carry more of them, further amplifying any individual's firepower potential.

CARTRIDGES

It also became possible to encapsulate the new propellants in easily handled metal cartridge cases. This had two results. One was that practical and reliable breech-loading mechanisms, such as bolt or falling block actions, could be devised and introduced. In turn, these led to a further quantum leap in individual firepower, especially after magazine rifles were introduced to replace single-shot, manually loaded rifles, greatly increasing the number of shots a soldier could deliver within a set time period. A well-trained musketeer could probably manage a steady two or three rounds a minute. Single-shot, breech-loading rifles could manage about eight, while for magazine rifles in trained hands, fifteen accurate rounds every minute became possible (in the British Army at least). The degree of firepower that even relatively small military formations could produce thus reached prodigious levels, and extended to combat ranges never before contemplated.

The attendant design and manufacturing techniques introduced by accurate machine tools were just as important to the evolution of the machine gun as metal cartridge cases and their smokeless contents. Thanks to all these technical innovations, a single firearm producing a constant stream of bullets became a practical proposition and the first true machine guns duly emerged. Infantry firepower could then reach new levels of lethality.

By the 1890s the first true machine guns were in the hands of the military. A single soldier could then deliver the firepower once produced by many. The drawback was that the commanding officers of the time did not know what to do with their new combat capabilities.

EARLY EXPERIENCES

The growing ascendancy and lethal properties of firepower, even as delivered by machine guns, took a long time to gain acceptance by the military mindset of European armed forces. The lethal capabilities of the rifle demonstrated during the American Civil War remained unappreciated by non-participant nations more interested in colonial campaigning than firepower demonstrations from a distant land. Even the lessons of the Franco-Prussian War of 1870–71, the first in which multiple-fire weapons were employed to any extent (the Mitrailleuse mle 1866), were either largely ignored or misunderstood. The South African Wars against the British at the end of the nineteenth century finally made at least some soldiers realize that firepower was ascendant, a lesson re-emphasized (but again either largely ignored or misunderstood) during the Russo-Japanese War of 1904–05. The old massed infantry tactics had to change drastically in the face of bolt action rifles. Organized defence from behind cover using infantry weapons alone could by then easily overcome frontal attack by infantry or cavalry.

The machine gun added further firepower potential to this situation. It took yet another dreadful war, the Great War of 1914–18, to place the properties of the machine gun into their proper tactical contexts. By 1918, the machine gun had achieved the tactical prominence it has yet to lose. The tragedy was that so many lives had to be lost before that prominence was finally appreciated and recognized.

STARTERS

Most accounts relating to the early development of the machine gun usually commence with mentions of early multiple-shot firearms. The customary histories of the first attempts start with the Puckle Gun proposals of the early eighteenth century and continue until the Gatling Gun, outlining all the numerous other forebears of today's machine guns. Most histories mention the French Mitrailleuse mle 1866, or the various 'organ guns', also known as *orgues* or *ribaudequins*.

Most of the early multiple-fire weapons were not true machine guns as we now know them. A handy (but by no means universally applicable) definition is that an authentic machine gun, once loaded, can automatically fire, eject the spent case, reload itself and fire again. This repetitive sequence is accomplished using the machine gun's own power without human intervention (other than aiming) for as long as a control device, typically a trigger, is kept actuated or until the ammunition supply runs out.

As will emerge, there are exceptions to this definition, but the main point is that the machine gun is a mechanical device that can operate under its own self-generated power. That power is usually derived from one of two sources. One is the recoil energy imparted as a cartridge is fired (recoil operation). The other comes from utilizing some of the energy produced by the propellant gases primarily intended to propel the projectile from the muzzle (gas operation). Externally powered machine guns are afforded their own chapter in this book.

The concept of producing some form of weapon that could supply multiple, rapidly fired projectiles to be directed towards an enemy dates back centuries. The suggestion pops up frequently in many old manuscripts and technical works relating to military matters, including those of Leonardo da Vinci. He, as with so many others of his time and after, was never able to transform theory into hardware, other than as some variant of the so-called organ guns, for one basic reason.

No matter how ingenious or futuristic their ideas were, the early rapid-fire prophets were limited in their practical achievements by the materials and manufacturing techniques then at their disposal. Early artillery and small arm

A typical, though rather late, example of an organ gun in the Brussels War Museum. The exact calibre was not displayed, but a breech closing system enabled all barrels to be loaded and unloaded together. This was almost certainly a fortification gun.

projectile-hurling systems involved black powder and the associated paper or fabric cartridges ignited by sparks or flame. Any alternative to the basic organ gun had to embrace some form of ammunition feed. The technology on hand at the time of the early theorists precluded any such arrangement. The corrosive residues of black powder would, in any case, soon render any feed devices unserviceable by fouling them solid after a few shots.

Organ guns, including the American Civil War's Requa Battery Gun (although there were many other similar examples dating back to the origins of gunpowder), were simply numerous individual barrels secured side by side on a frame (or banks of frames). Each barrel had to be loaded by hand, and that took time. Firing was carried out using a lever or crank handle; the earlier types employed flame or spark ignition. Requa guns, inevitably static due to their construction and weight, were employed by both sides during the American Civil War, usually covering the approaches to bridges or defiles, or as close-in defence measures for fortifications.

FEED SYSTEMS

By the time of the American Civil War, the first of what we now recognize as ammunition feed systems were being introduced, although for the time being they remained manually operated. One of them was the American Ager Gun, the so-called 'Coffee Mill' or 'Union Battery' gun. This had a hopper feed over the breech area, individual 0.58in rounds being mechanically fed into the breech by turning a crank handle. The Ager Gun certainly could work, but its loading efficiency and reliability were limited by the reloadable steel tube cartridges, all that were available at that time. Even so, it is on record that the Ager Gun could demonstrate a prolonged rate of fire sufficient to overheat dangerously the gun's single barrel.

Wilson Ager apparently sold fifty-four of his guns to the Union side, which, it is recorded, did not like or understand them. They were incorporated into the defences of Washington and, according to one reference, they were occasionally fired at Confederate positions along the Potomac River. If true, these firings probably marked the first use of any form of machine gun in conflict. After 1865, the Union Army disposed of its Ager Guns as rapidly as possible.

It took the invention of the so-called smokeless propellants before viable ammunition feed systems could be seriously considered. Smokeless propellants based on nitrocellulose and similar materials were much more powerful and energetic than any compound involving black powder. There was also another important advantage imparted by the new propellants. They tended to burn more slowly than black powder, providing a more gradual build-up in propellant gas production and power, in technical terms a smoother pressure curve. Black powder produced a very steep, stress-inducing pressure curve. Smokeless propellants took more time to burn completely so the rise in pressure was more gradual but very positive, enabling automatic mechanisms to operate more reliably and smoothly. They were also much 'cleaner', as they did not produce anywhere near the amounts of smoke and sticky residues, and the subsequent fouling, produced by black powder.

These innovations meant that relatively small amounts of propellant could be contained within the disposable cylindrical metal tubes known as cartridge cases, to be ignited (or primed) by substances that create heat when struck by a percussive device such as a firing pin. Metal cases and percussion ignition formed the keys to further automatic weapon developments as they could be made rugged enough to withstand mechanical handling. In addition, the close mechanical tolerances required to ensure that ammunition feed devices worked efficiently and reliably could be fabricated by the advanced industrial processes introduced towards the end of the nineteenth century.

Metal cases, smokeless propellants and percussion ignition were therefore the practical keys to further machine gun development. At first, metal cartridges (usually brass) were utilized with single-shot small arms such as breech-loading rifles and pistols. Their first applications to multiple-shot weapons were refinements of organ guns.

FRENCH MISTAKES

All early rapid/multiple-fire weapons were manually operated in some manner or other. The classic Mitrailleuse mle 1866 was originally an 1851 Belgian design by a Captain Fafschamps. It was later taken over by Joseph Montigny, by whom it was manufactured (with his name added) to defend Belgian fortifications, before being modified by the French Commandant Reffye and manufactured in great secrecy at the Meudon arsenal.

Although the original Montigny gun had thirty-seven barrels, the French mle 1866 consisted of a cluster of twenty-five barrels arranged around a central axis. Ammunition, secured in a single loading plate, was placed into the breech so that all the barrels were loaded simultaneously as a breech-closing lever was operated by hand. Further operation of a second lever fired each barrel in rapid succession. The plate then had to be removed, after reversing the breech lever (again by hand) before another loaded plate could be inserted ready for the next volley. There were several other contemporary guns operating along the same lines.

To complete the tale of the Mitrailleuse pattern weapons, it should be noted that they did not prosper under the battle conditions and attitudes encountered during the Franco-Prussian War of 1870–71. Loading, firing and unloading operations had to be carried out in a strict sequence that was often difficult to maintain in action, so jams were frequent. As a result, the optimum rates of fire were rarely achieved.

They were also misused tactically. Their weight meant that they had to be mounted on readily available field gun carriages, complete with ammunition carried in artillery-style limbers, and were then issued to field artillery batteries. Not surprisingly, they came to be regarded as some

Another denizen of the Brussels War Museum, a Belgian Montigny Mitrailleuse with thirty-seven barrels.

novel form of field artillery and were deployed accordingly, despite being considerably outranged by real field guns. When the Mitrailleuse was deployed alongside infantry it fared much better, but that did not happen often in 1870. Despite these perceived shortcomings, the French ordnance authorities persevered in further development from about 1872 onwards, although these efforts were soon terminated. The only relic of the Mitrailleuse-pattern weapons is that their name (originally denoting grapeshot) remains, to this day, the French term for the machine gun.

Period drawing of the French mle 1866 Mitrailleuse.

2   Gatling and Others

THE GATLING GUN

Although they were not true machine guns, the first manually operated, multiple-fire weapons (as opposed to the multi-barrelled organ guns) began to appear from about 1855 onwards. The Ager Gun has already been mentioned, as has the French Mitrailleuse family, but they were only two of many models either proposed or attempted around that period, most of them more optimistic than practical. Far more important in the longer term was the Gatling Gun.

The man who gave his name to a genre of rapid-firing weapons was Richard Jordan Gatling, born in North Carolina in 1818. After displaying an early aptitude for inventing items of farm machinery, resulting in considerable financial success, Gatling turned his attentions to a rapid-firing gun. By 1861, just in time for the American Civil War, Gatling had produced the prototype for a family of rapid-fire weapons that survive to this day. He patented the design the following year, but employment of the original production model by Union forces was limited. During the war, US Ordnance authorities were loath to introduce new and unknown weapons when all available production resources had to be applied to supplying items already established and understood. Their reluctance was no doubt reinforced by the early prototypes involving the loading of troublesome pre-loaded chambers instead of cartridge cases. The metal cartridge case was then not quite ready for reliable application. However, by 1865 most of its earlier shortcomings had been overcome, and the Gatling Gun appeared in discernible form.

Gatling Gun operations depended on two main features – multiple barrels and a cam-driven mechanism that loaded, fired and ejected cases. By actuating a single crank handle the barrels, usually six although some models had up to ten, rotated around a central axis. The same crank handle also drove a central rotor assembly on which a helical cam converted rotary motion into the reciprocal travel of a bolt. Each barrel had its own bolt within the rotor assembly, driven backwards and forwards by a cam on the bolt travelling within a fixed helical track. As each bolt and barrel rotated, a round was introduced to the gun mechanism, aligned with and then loaded into the barrel chamber. It then rotated within the barrel as the bolt moved forward to lock and fire the round by firing pin percussion at a fixed point in the rotary cycle. The bolt then withdrew to unlock, eject the spent case, and prepare to accept another round.

The main advantage of the Gatling system was that the feed, firing and ejection sequence was under complete mechanical control. Firing could continue as long as the crank handle was operated (or the ammunition supply lasted). Another advantage was that firing could continue for prolonged periods without dangerously overheating the barrels. Each loading/unloading sequence occupied an appreciable time so a degree of barrel cooling could take place between each barrel discharge.

Although technically sophisticated, the original Gatling Guns were still not true machine guns by this book's definition – their actions had to be driven manually. An 1890 US Navy exercise to

The Gardner gun

drive the gun using an electric motor eventually came to nothing and several decades were to elapse before the idea was resurrected. The modern electrically driven Gatlings are accorded their own chapter later in this book.

SALES SUCCESS

Appearing as it did just when improving manufacturing methods and cartridges cases were making an impact on small arms production, the Gatling Gun became a sales success, being sold to the US Army and Navy as well as exported to many overseas nations. For many recipients, however, the firepower advantages that the Gatling Gun could deliver were not immediately appreciated. Many nations at first diverted their new toys to colonial warfare, while others, despite the lessons of the Franco-Prussian War, regarded the

Gatling as a form of field artillery. The latter assumption proved to be very wrong, for early Gatling Guns were chambered for what were essentially infantry calibres, with correspondingly limited ranges. When Gatlings were deployed alongside and in support of infantry their true worth soon became very apparent.

Once the Gatling Gun had become established, it was developed through a number of models. As a general rule, infantry weapon calibres grew smaller with the increased power of modern smokeless propellants, so Gatling Gun calibres decreased accordingly. Gun models gradually became more compact and lighter, usually firing the same rifle cartridges as the infantry of the nation involved. Various types of ammunition feed were introduced, from simple vertical hoppers to large capacity drums. The early field gun wheeled carriages gradually gave way to smaller and lighter tripods, or pivot mountings on ships, although the USA retained some field carriages until the guns they carried were retired.

Gatling copies abounded, despite Gatling's carefully guarded patents. Perhaps the most important was the Gorloff Gun, a direct copy of the Gatling produced in Russia following the initial sale of a batch of 400 guns and a subsequent licence production agreement to build more within Russia. Gatling Guns were also produced under licence in Austria for a while, although those went mainly to Turkey. Far more important numerically was the licence agreement made with the Armstrong Company of the United Kingdom. Armstrong manufactured Gatling Guns in many calibres and forms, many for export, and their Gatlings were widely employed by the British Army and Royal Navy, especially for colonial warfare where they proved ideal for destroying attacking hordes.

In 1888, the European patent rights for the Gatling Gun were purchased by one Frederick Penfield, again of the United Kingdom, although it is doubtful if the costs involved were ever recovered. From 1890 onwards the Gatling Gun became increasingly obsolescent. Fully automatic machine guns had appeared by then, the Maxim Gun taking over markets once dominated by the Gatling. By about 1900 few nations retained the Gatling Gun, other than as reserve weapons.

Yet the Gatling Gun did not just fade away. The last recorded variant was the US Army's Model 1903, manufactured for Gatling by Colt's. It was an updated version of the earlier Model 1900, chambered to accept the then newly adopted 0.30-06 Springfield rifle cartridge. The last of them was not delivered until 1907. It was 1911 before the US Army officially withdrew the last Gatlings from its inventory, although some remained in odd corners. Perhaps the last probable mention of manually operated Gatlings in service came during the Korean War when reports were made of at least one still in front-line action with the Communist Chinese. However, these latter reports have proved difficult to verify. If true, they were probably Russian Gorloff Guns.

Gatling himself died in 1903. His gun was to remain out of production for well over four decades before a new Gatling Gun generation arose. These are covered in Chapter 22.

The Gatling Gun	
Model	Gatling (typical)
Calibre	12.7mm (0.50in)
Length	not recorded
Weight	363kg (800lb)
Muzzle velocity	not recorded
Rate of fire	60rds/min
Feed	gravity

NORDENFELDT

Gatling was always prepared to protect his patents, so any aspiring machine-gun manufacturer had to avoid utilizing anything even remotely similar to the Gatling mechanisms – unless they wanted to spend time in court. One innovation unlikely to infringe any patent appeared during the early 1860s, namely the Claxton gun. This had two barrels and two sliding breech mechanisms set on a frame. As the operator worked a horizontal handle from side to side, the breeches were moved to one side for loading and then, when the lever was moved to the other side, the spent cases were ejected, the actual firing taking place when the lever was in the central position. The faster the operator worked the lever, the greater the cyclic firing rate, the maximum possible being about 80rds/min, although the rate could be erratic.

The Claxton was not a success, being judged as too fragile for anything other than a demonstration model. Although there was probably no connection, during the 1870s a Swedish engineer, Helge Palmcrantz, devised a similar mechanism. His early attempts involved multiple barrels arranged horizontally and side by side, as required, so that rounds could be fed under gravity from vertical hoppers into each barrel via a series of breech blocks that opened and closed under the control of a single manually operated lever. An extra locking mechanism containing the firing pins was inserted behind the barrels to fire them all in a rapid sequence rather than in a volley. In effect, the Palmcrantz mechanism was an updated organ gun, but with the refinement that rapid reloading was possible and single shots could be selected.

As so often happens in the field of invention, Palmcrantz was a better engineer than businessman and lacked the funding necessary to manufacture and sell his design. Finance eventually came from a Swedish, London-based financier named Thorsten Wilhelm Nordenfeldt. In return for his largesse he agreed to manufacture and market the gun – provided it bore his name. The name Palmcrantz therefore faded from the scene, although it may still be encountered in some technical references.

Nordenfeldt was considerably assisted in his sales efforts by the issue of a machine-gun requirement for the British Army and Admiralty.

A typical 0.45in Nordenfeldt Gun as used by the British Admiralty.

Their 1880 outline specifications could be readily met by the Nordenfeldt machine gun, especially as the requirement asked for a cyclic fire rate of 400rds/min or over, preferably not from a single barrel. Since the hand-operated Nordenfeldt mechanism could manage up to 1,200rds/min in the hands of a skilled operator (considerably assisted by the provision of ten barrels), it could fulfil the requirements. In addition, manufacturing could take place within the UK. A refinement on some Nordenfeldt models was that the barrels could be arranged in an adjustable frame so that the fire of all barrels would converge at a central point at whatever range was selected.

At that time, most armed forces advocated volley fire from multiple barrels, rather than reliance on fire from a single barrel, so the Nordenfeldt Gun met contemporary needs exactly. Guns were produced on field carriages, as well as various pivot mountings for use on naval vessels, many adorned with solid and heavy aiming mechanisms. Apart from Nordenfeldt's vigorous selling techniques, sales were no doubt assisted by a high standard of manufacture and the lavish provision of brass and other metals that could be highly polished, a feature that no doubt engendered much satisfaction in the military minds of the period.

Nordenfeldt factories were established in Spain and Sweden as well as in the UK. During the late 1880s and the 1890s the Nordenfeldt concern offered some eighteen models, from rifle calibres up to 37mm, all of them notable for their substantial and sturdy construction. The number of barrels on some models was as many as ten; others had from two to five. One notable Nordenfeldt offering was what we would now term a light machine gun. This had a single barrel with a single lever and toggle lock to be cranked to and fro by hand to carry out the loading, locking and ejection operations. One feature of this weapon was that the bolt head rotated for locking, something way ahead of its time and the system now almost universally employed on modern automatic rifles and machine guns. While hardly capable of sustained fire, due to the manual operation limiting discharges to a cyclic maximum of 180 rds/min, the single barrel Nordenfeldt Gun weighed 5.9kg (13lb), little more than a contemporary service rifle.

There were no takers for the light model, however, the philosophy of the time favouring multiple-barrelled weapons. In fact, the Nordenfeldt era soon ended. Its manually operated mechanism was outdated almost as soon as it appeared, overtaken by the automatic machine gun in its many forms. Nevertheless, Nordenfeldt Guns remained in service until the early 1900s before being discarded, most of them still as good as new thanks to their high standard of manufacture.

There was one final and extremely odd item to emerge under the Nordenfeldt name. It appeared in 1897, designed by one Captain W. Bergman of the Swedish Army (not to be confused with the German Bergmann). It was unique in being operated either manually or automatically. Bergman sold his patent to Nordenfeldt, to whom the option of manual operation still appealed – many observers of the time were convinced that automatic machine guns would never catch on.

For automatic fire, the gun operated using a form of recoil actuation coupled with a system of carefully machined rollers and levers to operate the bolt, locking and loading sequences. For manual control, a fire selector switch lever enabled the same mechanisms to be operated by a crank handle on the right of the receiver. The gun was water-cooled, was loaded from an advanced metal link ammunition feed and had an automatic cyclic rate of fire of 600rds/min. It appears that only one example of this hybrid was made.

GARDNER

As will become apparent throughout this book, Americans have always been well to the fore in just about every aspect of machine-gun development. This applied to manually operated guns as well as other types, the names of Gatling, Ager and Claxton being among those already mentioned.

Another American who found more success abroad than in his own country was William Gardner of Toledo, Ohio. He was yet another small-arms inventor who lacked development capital. Following experience of Gatling Guns during the Civil War, he decided he could do better. By 1874 he had devised the mechanism for a manually operated machine gun. In order to get his design manufactured he sold the patent rights to Pratt & Whitney of Hartford, Connecticut (later better known for aircraft engines), in exchange for royalty payments on future sales.

Gardner's basic mechanism was simple. It consisted of two parallel barrels, each with its own bolt. By turning a side-mounted handle in the same manner as a barrel organ, the movement would keep the two bolts 180 degrees out of phase with each other. As one bolt was forward in the locking and firing position the other was fully to the rear ready for loading, after having ejected the previous spent case during its rearward travel. Turning the handle reversed the process. Ammunition feed problems were minimized by innovations devised by Pratt & Whitney engineers, who also virtually perfected the mechanism. Instead of merely relying on gravity to feed rounds from a

vertical hopper over the receiver, each round was positively fed into its final feed position by a system of cams, levers and sprockets. Another innovation was a positive method of extracting spent cases from the chamber.

The Gardner Gun, still bearing it's originator's name, was extensively tested by the US Navy during 1880, firing thousands of rounds without serious stoppages other than allowing the barrels to cool after prolonged firings. Despite emphatic official acknowledgements that the gun was reliable, simple and relatively light, it was not adopted. The US armed forces had already invested in the Gatling and did not have any immediate requirement for anything else. Pratt & Whitney therefore lost interest in the Gardner project.

Gardner then turned his attentions to the United Kingdom. There the Admiralty was considering the adoption of machine guns, even though Nordenfeldt and Gatling had already made inroads into that market. Further extensive and (for their time) demanding trials completed during 1881 re-emphasized the reliability of the Gardner Gun, so it was adopted by the British Admiralty who came to regard it as the best weapon of its kind available at that time. Yet despite considerable efforts, the 'British' Gardner Gun achieved no significant sales elsewhere, other than to the Italian Navy. The Löwe concern of Berlin obtained a European licence to manufacture the Gardner Gun, but apart from sales of a small batch to Switzerland, the results were few.

The Gardner Gun was produced in quantity for the Royal Navy in several forms. A barrel-cooling water jacket was added on some models, a feature that by itself demonstrated the firepower production potential of Gardner's design, while another model demonstrated that the Gardner mechanism could also be employed to drive a single-barrel model. To make the Gardner Gun more portable for land operations in remote regions, a Royal Navy engineer devised a light tripod mounting, doing away with the field carriage and ammunition limber normally employed.

A twin-barrel Gardner Gun – note the lavish use of expensive highly polished brass and bronze.

When smokeless propellants became more widely used, a belt-fed ammunition system was introduced. By the time it had been added, a new name, that of Robertson, had been applied to the gun. However, by that stage the manually operated Gardner/Robertson Gun had been superseded by the automatic machine guns, so the belt-fed model could not prosper.

THE OTHER OTHERS

The above listing covers the main manually operated machine-gun innovators, although the register could be continued for several pages. In keeping with the Yankee 'can do' ingenuity of the latter decades of the late nineteenth century, most of the 'other' names were American. They included Winder, Bailey, Williams, Taylor, Farwell and Lowell. There were many others.

The Gardner Gun	
Model	Gardner
Calibre	11.43mm (0.45in)
Length	not recorded
Weight	*c.* 180kg (400lb)
Muzzle velocity	420m/s (1,280ft/sec)
Rate of fire	60rds/min
Feed	gravity

All these names had one thing in common (apart from being American) in that their designs were not deemed successful, either mechanically or commercially, and so fell by the wayside. Their names have now faded into ordnance history.

3 Maxim

In 1881 it seemed that just about every inventor and engineer in Europe was searching for a way to produce a truly automatic machine gun. That was the conclusion reached by one Hiram Stevens Maxim soon after he arrived in Europe from his native USA in order to research various European electrical patents for possible commercial exploitation back home. In 1881 Maxim was only forty-one years old and unqualified in any form of gunmaking or design. Neither was he formally qualified in anything else, but he was blessed with an enquiring and inventive mind.

From a young age Maxim had virtually educated himself in whatever field he was then engaged, from carriage-building to signwriting, before eventually venturing into the realm of electric lighting. Throughout his career, Maxim consistently displayed a remarkable aptitude for inventing things that were both practical and utilitarian, ranging from a resettable mousetrap to a system of automatic fire-suppression water sprinklers still in use today. Other inventions included a novel form of classroom blackboard paint, improved combustible gas- or steam-driven machinery, and much else besides. As he progressed, Maxim learned the value of securing patents for his many inventions, in the process earning himself a dependable living, a long way removed from his early days back on the family farm in Dexter, Maine.

In 1882, Maxim made his first forays into the machine-gun world. Having received no formal technical education he was unfettered by any of the established engineering conventions, and so approached the challenge of inventing a practical machine gun with a completely open mind.

THE FIRST GUN

Maxim's approach started by appreciating that some form of internally generated power had to be involved, which, for him, meant the propelling gases created on firing. Like so many others of his time he had noted that discharging a firearm produced so much recoil, or 'kick', that shoulders could be bruised. Why not harness that energy to power a mechanism?

Maxim was probably not alone in that realization, but he did make a mechanism that worked. He started by designing a semi-automatic rifle, more as a test bed than as a serious gun venture. Firing his design pushed a spring-loaded butt plate held against a shoulder. The plate transmitted much of the firing energy back to a series of reloading levers. Having accomplished that and determined that recoil forces could drive a gun mechanism, Maxim decided that he could advance his recoil-based ideas still further. Gradually, electrical devices occupied less and less of Maxim's time as he increasingly devoted his inventive attentions to a machine gun.

Operating from a small factory at a now-unlikely address in Hatton Garden, London, Maxim devised and operated his own machine tools to construct various mechanisms based on recoil principles until one worked to his satisfaction. His practical experience meant that he could

Hidden away in a Pretoria workshop, this early Maxim was reportedly involved in the infamous Jameson Raid of early 1896.

carry out all the many design stages, from working drawings to making the tools to fabricate and machine components. By 1884 his first prototype, chambered to fire the then-current 0.45in British service rifle cartridge, was ready for demonstration. The only part not produced under Maxim auspices was the barrel.

Many of the features of that first prototype, the first automatic machine gun, remained unique to it, one being a mechanism that could regulate the rate of fire from a single shot every minute to as many as 600rds/min – it proved unnecessary other than as a sales gimmick. But the basic operating mechanism of that first prototype was to remain virtually unaltered from then onwards.

RECOIL OPERATION

What was to become universally known as the Maxim Gun had a single barrel held in a jacket with front and rear bearings. At the instant of firing the barrel was locked to a bolt (or perhaps bolt block would be a better term), so that the firing recoil forces could drive both to the rear. After a short travel, during which the bullet had

left the muzzle and chamber pressures had fallen to a safe level, further barrel movement was arrested, leaving the bolt to travel on towards the rear, accelerated by the lever action and control of a cammed, downwards-folding toggle lock. At the end of the bolt travel, a coiled fusee spring, tensioned during the rearward movement, drove the bolt forward again, feeding a round in the process. The final operation was chambering and locking a fresh round in the barrel chamber, ejecting the spent cartridge case as it did so. If the trigger was kept depressed the cycle could then be repeated. The recoil and return-spring power were also employed to actuate the ammunition feed. Maxim devised both drum magazine and ammunition belt-feed systems, but in the event only the belt feed was selected, originally with 333-round fabric belts capable of being linked together to maintain fire over long periods. Cocking (or charging) the gun was accomplished using a cranking handle on the right-hand side of the receiver. The cyclic rate of fire varied with the power of the cartridge involved, but was usually about 600rds/min.

Maxim's mechanism was far more complex than indicated by the above short outline, which

Soldiers of the 1st Battalion Princess of Wales' Own Yorkshire Regiment (The Green Howards) on field exercises with their Maxim Guns at the Curragh in 1896.

does not include the process of locking and firing. From the prototype onwards, the entire system featured numerous ingenious touches that required little subsequent modification. Once the gun had passed the initial prototype stage, the only enhancements were devoted to reducing overall weight and making the mechanism 'soldier friendly'. Access to all parts for repair or maintenance was made easy and simple to the point where any soldier could be taught the procedures. For instance, the bolt and lock could be rapidly removed or replaced by hand and without recourse to tools. Later models were provided with a muzzle attachment that provided extra 'push to the rear' for the barrel and bolt on firing. The barrel jackets were also arranged to contain water for barrel cooling. This latter option eventually became a fixture on most service models, although a few remained air-cooled.

MANUFACTURING

If the early Maxim Guns had any shortcomings it was that they were heavy. They also took a great deal of time to manufacture. The weight problem, compounded by many components being machined from solid steel or bronze, was accommodated on early models by mounting them on light, horse-drawn field artillery carriages for land service or on pivot mountings for use at sea. Later, lighter models mounted on tripods that could be carried by infantry or on pack animals were introduced. The bugbear of machine guns, namely the weight and bulk of sufficient ammunition to supply the gun for viable combat periods, had yet to be addressed. Ammunition supply for machine guns was then, as now, a logistic problem yet to be satisfactorily solved.

The manufacturing problem was not foreseen or appreciated during the nineteenth century. At that time, skilled artisans were in fairly plentiful supply, while time lavished in the factory never seemed to be a drawback. Craftsmen, including gunmakers, wanted to display their skills. The time problem arose only later, when massed production requirements were imposed. There was also the unstated fact that time-demanding, hand-fitted precision could produce a 'value-added' factor reflected in the price ticket and subsequent profits, another factor still with us today.

The initial Maxim Gun models employed black powder cartridges. Once smokeless propellants were introduced the Maxim mechanism was able to work even better, since, thanks to the smoother pressure curve on firing, many of the firing stresses could be significantly reduced, while operation became smoother. In addition, the mechanism was less exposed to fouling. In time, the Maxim Gun was produced to fire just about every European service rifle cartridge then extant, the basic weapon being scaled up to calibres of 37mm or even 40mm, the former being the so-called Pom-Poms of the Boer War and after.

SELLING THE GUN

The main reason for the array of calibres was to support Maxim's dynamic salesmanship, which reached just about every corner of Europe. Wherever he travelled, Maxim pitched his sales at the highest executive levels possible, including to many of the crowned heads of Europe. Being a practical man, Maxim gave numerous firing demonstrations, many of them devouring thousands of rounds. In the process, he indicated to

any other hopeful designers that his gun was the one that would dominate the marketplace for automatic weapons. He also emphasized that, with the arrival of the Maxim Gun, the brief era of the manually operated machine gun was over.

Maxim also employed his fertile mind to contemplate just about every other system capable of producing automatic fire, and, by 1885, he had patented many of them as well, all in addition to the numerous master patents associated with his own gun. The Maxim Gun was thus able to lead the international machine-gun market for decades.

Starting in 1887, Italy and Austria were the first purchasers of the Maxim Gun. Orders for the Maxim Gun then increased to a flood, so much so that the capacity of the Hatton Garden facility, little more than a workshop, was soon exceeded. A move was therefore made to a new factory at Crayford in Kent. An association with the Nordenfeldt concern, formed primarily in order to utilize the production capacity of the Nordenfeldt factories, proved to be relatively short-lived, although it did result in the weapon sales services of Basil Zaharoff being transferred to the Maxim. Far more enduring was the long-standing affiliation with the giant Vickers military engineering

A typical example of a commercial Maxim-Nordenfeldt machine gun – note the seat on the tripod leg.

British Army Maxims on show on Malta, 1897.

concern, finally resulting in the establishment of Vickers Sons & Maxim Limited in 1897, with super-salesman Zaharoff still in train.

The British armed forces became exponents of the Maxim Gun from 1891 onwards, even if it was usually relegated to colonial campaigning. A few were diverted to the defence of harbours against the new-fangled motor torpedo boat. Most UK-based senior officers regarded their new Maxim Guns as little more than toys and largely relegated them to fortifications, thwarting the suppressed enthusiasms of the many junior officers who realized the tactical potential of the gun, but remained quiet to avoid damaging their long-term service careers. Elsewhere, other nations were more forward-looking. Nations such as Germany, Russia and Switzerland adopted the Maxim Gun with alacrity and went to the extent of making licence production arrangements, of which more in the following chapters.

The one nation that did not take to the Maxim Gun was the USA. Despite numerous impressive demonstrations made from 1888 onwards, sales of a 37mm model were made only to the US Navy. The Navy took about 100 examples and retained them until the 1920s. But US Army ordnance procurement authorities remained unenthusiastic. They already had the Gatling Gun, which seemed to meet all their requirements, money was tight, and they also preferred a home-grown design

rather than something from across the water, a factor reinforced by Maxim becoming a naturalized British subject in 1900. It was 1904 before the US Army realized how far behind it had fallen in military technology. Only then did the US Army adopt 282 examples of the last production version of the Maxim Gun, the 0.30 Model 1904.

FINAL DAYS

During the 1890s the American rejections mattered little commercially. Orders continued to arrive from all over the world and continued after the last purely Maxim model had appeared. It was, as mentioned above, the Model 1904. Some years later (1911), and following expansion of his interests into the realm of 'heavier than air flying machines', Sir Hiram Maxim retired (he had been knighted in 1901 'for services to the British Empire'). By then he had also dabbled with sound suppressors (silencers) for small arms. His final sound-reducing design, developed in association with one of his sons, became the standard for all the similar designs that followed.

On his retirement all rights to the Maxim Gun were taken over by Vickers, and Maxim's name was removed from the renamed Vickers Limited letterheads. With the Maxim patents having lapsed with time, Vickers introduced its own modifications by inverting the Maxim toggle lock and introducing extra measures to reduce the weight of the entire design. The Maxim Gun then became the Vickers Gun, a weapon that also deserves its own chapter in this book (*see* Chapter 7).

Sir Hiram Maxim died in 1916 and was thus unfortunate enough to act as a distant witness to the slaughter his genius had made possible. Perhaps his most lasting memorial is that his gun mechanism remains virtually unchanged to this day, despite many attempts at enhancement over the years. Maxim Guns are very rarely encountered now (if at all), those few being almost without exception of Russian/Soviet Union origin.

The Maxim Gun

Model	Maxim (typical)
Calibre	11.43mm (0.45in)
Length	*c.* 1,160mm (45.7in)
Weight	27.2kg (60lb)
Muzzle velocity	364m/s (1,200ft/sec)
Rate of fire	600rds/min
Feed	333-round belt

4 German Maxims

In addition to his many technical skills and aptitudes, Hiram Maxim also proved to be remarkably astute when it came to business matters. Having been disadvantaged by others taking over his ideas during his early life, Maxim soon came to appreciate the power of patents and the importance of guarding them closely. Thus, even before he started work on his machine gun, he was already established financially. He went on to become extremely rich, although there were to be a few sticky corporate patches as Maxim-associated companies came and went.

Not all of Maxim's gun income came from direct sales. A sizeable initial export sale often led to licensed production in the customer's country, together with some form of royalty arrangement. A continuity of income was then assured.

LICENCES

Among these many licence production agreements, the one concluded with Germany must have been comfortably profitable. Two agreements were involved. The first was with the mighty Krupps concern, then the largest armament manufacturers in Europe. In 1888 Krupps took out a twenty-year agreement to produce the Maxim Gun, but subsequently never did so. Exactly why is now not known, although by the end of the 1900s Krupps was manufacturing 37mm Maxim Pom-Poms for the German Navy. But the 1888 agreement did not result in any land-based Maxim Gun production, although a large potential market existed in Germany for rifle-calibre machine guns.

According to legend, the Kaiser himself was the first to purchase Maxim Guns for his personal Dragoon Guard regiments, using his own private funds. Exactly why the anticipated production for the rest of the German Army did not initially materialize is still uncertain. It appears to have been at least partly due to the reluctance of some senior Krupps executives to start dabbling in rifle-calibre weapons (they normally specialized in field and heavy artillery). The Maxim concern therefore turned to one Sigmund Löwe, who had become involved with Maxim during that company's association with Nordenfeldt. Löwe (often Anglicized as Loewe) had an elder brother, Ludwig, who owned a Berlin-centred precision engineering concern, originally established to manufacture sewing machines, but which had subsequently entered the field of ammunition and armaments production.

By late 1892 a seven-year licence agreement had been established between the Löwe and Maxim concerns. A few pattern guns were sent to Berlin and production of German guns commenced there in 1894. By 1897 Löwe was becoming so involved with gun production, including ammunition, Mauser rifles and various pistols, that he was instrumental in the establishment of a new concern, the Deutsche Waffen und Munitions Fabriken, soon familiar to many as DWM.

DWM

By 1899 the old licence agreement with Vickers-Maxim had lapsed and was not renewed, although royalties continued to be paid for some years. By then, DWM was a Maxim Gun producer on a major scale, marketing its output not just to the German Army and Navy, but to many overseas countries as well, competing with the Vickers-Maxim concern and, by then, several other machine-gun manufacturers. Early DWM sales successes included to Bulgaria, China, Romania, Russia, Serbia, Turkey and several others, customers that might have once been thought committed to British Maxim Guns.

The then expanding German Navy adopted DWM Maxims as early as 1894 – its initial order was one factor involved in the establishment of DWM. By contrast, and in common with many other European nations, the German Army hierarchy was at first reluctant to purchase any form of machine gun. In 1870–71 a few Mitrailleuse-pattern weapons had been fielded by Bavarian contingents, but they were not deployed in an intelligent manner and were later categorized as a failure. That bad reputation lingered for many years, as a result of which the German General Staff spent little time considering machine guns. Those staff officers were at least partially converted when Maxim Guns were demonstrated to them. To investigate their potential, the Army formed machine-gun detachments charged with determining how the new guns could be best deployed in future actions. During 1899 the Army purchased its first DWM Maxim model, the Maschinengewehr 99, or MG99.

The MG99 had much in common with the German Navy's Model 1894, but introduced a novel mounting unlike anything else. This was the *Schlittenlafette*, or sledge mount, destined to become a German machine-gun recognition feature. This was a sturdy steel contrivance that provided a firm mounting once in action, but for moves it could either be folded flat and dragged along the ground by two or more soldiers, or carried between two like a stretcher. Two wheels could be added if required. For longer moves wheeled transport carriages and pack-horse harnesses were devised. Ammunition was also dragged on sledges.

The Maschinengewehr 99, or MG99, on display. The MG99 had much in common with the German Navy's Model 1894 but introduced a novel mounting unlike anything else. This was the first Schlittenlafette.

The *Schlittenlafette*, with small modifications, was carried over to the next DWM model, the MG01, the main change on the gun being that the original heavy brass barrel-cooling water jacket changed to steel.

NEW MODELS

During 1904 and 1905 the Russo-Japanese War demonstrated the full killing potential of the Maxim Gun. Russian Maxims (*see* Chapter 5) repeatedly cut swathes through the persistently attacking Japanese infantry to the extent that the conflict became bogged down in siege-and-trench warfare a decade before the rest of the world came to dread the power of the machine gun. The war involved the toleration of enormous casualties, with the result that, until the end, the Russian Maxims continued to take their lethal toll, not forgetting the equally lethal efficiency of the Japanese Hotchkiss guns.

As was the custom in those days, the Russo-Japanese War was attended by many foreign observers, amongst whom the Germans were notable by their dedication to tactical detail. Unlike many other observers who dismissed the events of 1904–05 as not applicable to European wars, the German observers took careful notes, among which the lethality of the Maxim Gun featured prominently. When the observers' reports were received in Berlin, the General Staff responded with speed. A completely new approach to machine-gun warfare was prepared.

Machine guns became an infantry priority. Every battalion came to have its own highly trained machine-gun detachments, who, at first, worked out their own tactics and fire control along with appropriate field fortification techniques and all the other minutiae of their future tasks. The General Staff also observed how other European nations were organizing their machine guns and adopted many of their ideas, including from British Army machine-gun units when they were still in the planning stage. Thus when the Great War commenced in 1914 the German Army was probably the best-prepared machine-gun exponent among the combatant forces.

sMG08

By 1914 the German Army had a new Maxim Gun, the sMG08 (schwere Maschinen Gewehr 08, with the 'schwere' (s) denoting heavy) firing the standard German 7.92 × 57mm rifle cartridge. The sMG08 differed from earlier models mainly by being lighter. Until 1908 the German Army had accepted that machine guns were heavy, but its future plans envisaged the need for a high degree of tactical mobility. By replacing many of the original Maxim components with lighter steels, and making other changes, the gun weight was reduced significantly, from about 26kg (57.3lb) to around 16.5kg (36.4lb), without affecting reliability. The same attentions were applied to the *Schlittenlafette*, reducing the weight of that hefty assembly from 56kg (123.5lb) to about 24kg (53lb). Another change came with the introduction of optical sights for firing at long-range targets and the first dial (or panoramic) sights for indirect fire against distant targets.

The most significant post-1908 change came with production. The German Army demanded huge numbers of machine guns (by contemporary standards) and issued them freely. By 1914 the Army had just over 4,400, a very respectable holding for the time. By the end of 1918 DWM production had reached approximately 50,000, with another 22,000 or so being made by the Königliche Gewehr und Munitionsfabrik at Spandau, Berlin. The bulk of these totals was manufactured during 1917 and 1918.

ORGANIZATION AND TACTICS

In addition to the machine-gun companies within every infantry regiment, each with an establish-

British soldiers turning a captured MG08 against its former owners.

ment (often exceeded) of six guns, the German Army also formed special six-gun machine-gun detachments to act as independent batteries under instructions from higher command levels. As machine guns were regarded as expendable infantry weapons, reserve guns at the rate of one gun to every six were held close to the front lines to replace losses in action.

As important as their numbers, was the way in which the sMG08s were used. Wherever possible,

they were sited in pairs to provide interlocking fields of fire, to the flanks (again wherever possible), and to maximize shock-and-fire effects. By 1918, sMG08s were only rarely deployed in forward trench lines. Instead, they were carefully emplaced just behind the first defence line in such a manner that their field of fire was the maximum that could be achieved, wherever possible having the all-important interlocking with fields of fire from other weapons nearby. Just as important as opening fire was holding fire until the maximum results could be achieved. The main point is that the sMG08 was only rarely used in isolation, multi-gun deployments being preferred.

Great attention was also given to protection for the guns and their valuable crews. By 1918 concrete pillbox structures specially built for machine guns were a common sight among the German defences, while guns in more exposed positions were provided with sandbag or earth revetments.

For the German Army, the key to the optimum employment of machine guns was thorough and careful training for the gun crews and their officers. This took time and the unsparing expenditure of ammunition, even as late as 1918. As a result, gun crew casualties became difficult to replace so, with time, the availability of special body armour, including special helmets (with armoured visors) and breastplates, further protected them. Some guns gained further protection from extra shields, while an armoured steel disc behind the muzzle became a frequent addition to protect the barrel jacket from frontal fire.

The German sMG08 came to dominate the Western Front battlefields of the Great War. They were largely responsible for the slaughter at Loos (1915), the Somme (1916) and the Third Battle of Ypres (1917), to mention just British Army battles. They also ruled the battlefields of the Eastern Front from 1914 to 1917.

The sMG08	
Model	sMG08
Calibre	7.92mm (0.312in)
Length	1,175mm (46.25in)
Weight	62kg (137lb)
Muzzle velocity	900m/s (2,925ft/sec)
Rate of fire	300–450rds/min
Feed	250-round belt

leMG08/15

By 1917, an important variant of the sMG08 had appeared. Spurred on by encounters with Lewis Guns, the German technical staff determined to produce a more portable version of the sMG08, any alternative type of gun being rejected to minimize the disruption of already established production facilities. Although the German Army employed as many Lewis Guns as could be captured or recovered from the battlefields, it could not depend on a regular supply. Some existing product had to be selected for conversion. It therefore had to be a lightened sMG08 or nothing for a long while.

The 'light' gun duly appeared in the form of the leMG08/15 (le – *leichte* – light), which was supposed to be carried and fired by one man. This was a version of the sMG08 with a bipod in place of the former heavy mounting arrangements, plus a shoulder stock and a pistol grip and trigger. The barrel jacket was slimmer and provision was made for a side-mounted drum for 100-round fabric ammunition belts. Despite all the efforts involved, the end result was still a heavy and clumsy machine gun that, at about 19.5kg (43lb) complete with bipod, could just about be carried and operated by a single soldier – but he had to be strong.

The intention was that the leMG08/15 would be issued at the rate of two to every infantry platoon, where they could considerably enhance the unit's firepower. To achieve this, seven separate factories became involved. Between them, they had produced about 130,000 guns by the time the war ended. That total was further enlarged by the adoption of the leMG08/15 as the LMG08/15 (the L denotes *Luft* – air), a standard weapon for the German Air Force, although these guns had their jackets perforated for air cooling, plus some other modifications to suit their airborne fixed installations. There was also the ground-based leMG08/18, a variant of the leMG08/15 with the barrel jacket slotted to provide air cooling for the barrel. The intention was to provide a lighter model of the leMG08/15, but few were made

The unfortunate early attempt at a light machine gun, the 7.92mm leMG08/15.

The leMG08/15	
Model	leMG08/15
Calibre	7.92mm (0.312in)
Length	1,400mm (57in)
Weight	18kg (39lb) unloaded
Muzzle velocity	900m/s (2,925ft/sec)
Rate of fire	300–450rds/min
Feed	100-round belt

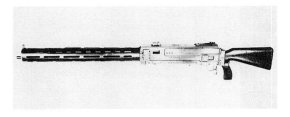

Lightweight Maxim, the DMW 7.9mm leMG14 Parabellum, used primarily as an aircraft weapon.

before the war ended and the project was not continued after 1918.

To return to the sMG08, that too began to adopt new roles. One was as an air defence weapon, various types of high angle mounting being devised and produced. The sMG08 also featured as the secondary armament of the first German tank, the A7V. Those lumbering leviathans carried no less than six sMG08s, their crews operating in cramped and awkward conditions.

PARABELLUM

One offshoot of German Maxim development was a machine gun usually known simply as the Parabellum, a name apparently derived from the telegraph address of DWM, where the gun was made. It started life as a DWM private venture intended to investigate the possibilities of a gun much lighter than the usual Maxims, originally for ground service. When requests for aircraft armament started to appear from about 1910 onwards, the concept was revisited by one Karl Heinemann, a DWM engineer.

As lightness was the driving force behind the project, Heinemann concentrated on an air-cooled weapon on which everything possible was done to reduce weight, while retaining the well-known Maxim operating principles. Heinemann decided to save receiver weight and space by inverting the

Maxim toggle lock in exactly the same manner as for the British Vickers Gun (*see* Chapter 7).

The resultant Parabellum, or leMG14, was produced for both fixed and flexible aircraft installations. A leMG14/17 had a shorter barrel and a reduced diameter barrel jacket to assist handling in slipstreams, plus provision for an optical sight. Flexible installation guns for observers or airships were given shoulder stocks, pistol grips and belts fed from ammunition drums. Fixed applications were often supplied with belts holding hundreds of rounds. The rate of fire was between 650 and 750rds/min, which was really too slow for airborne combat by 1918, so after then the Parabellum swiftly vanished from the scene.

MORE SERVICE

After 1918, the terms of the Treaty of Versailles limited the size of the German Army to 100,000 men. They were allowed to retain 861 heavy and

1,475 light machine guns. Needless to say, totals well above the imposed quantities were spirited away from the gaze of Treaty observers, along with spares and accessories, to be clandestinely stockpiled against some future use. Further guns were claimed as Allied war booty. Light and heavy guns went to Belgium and Poland, with more going to the new Baltic States and Yugoslavia. Yet more were sold around the world on commercial terms. Any guns left over from these exercises were either scrapped or distributed as war trophies.

As early as 1918 German planners had determined that their future machine guns would be of the air-cooled, general-purpose type and, in time, these duly appeared (*see* Chapter 16). In the meantime, the attenuated Reichswehr had to make do with the sMG08 and leMG08/15. Those two machine guns were the ones that many German soldiers trained with during the inter-war years and by 1939 the sMG08 and leMG08/15 were still significant items within the new Wehrmacht inventory. However, by then the MG34 had

appeared, and as early as 1936 had assumed most of the combat roles once shouldered by the old Maxim Guns.

There were still useful roles for the old guns to perform. Swelled by quantities of guns originally distributed as war reparations after 1918, only to change hands once again following the German victories of 1939–41, the ageing Maxims fulfilled combat tasks along the Atlantic Wall coastal defences and other fortifications. Many garrison units in occupied territories retained both the sMG08 and leMG08/15 until the end in 1945, by which time any remaining stockpiled guns had been passed to the hapless Volksturm home defence units meant to act as last-ditch defenders of the Third Reich.

CALIBRE FOOTNOTES

The sMG08 and leMG08/15 were chambered for 7.92 × 57mm ammunition, but other calibres appeared. One came after 1918 when captured weapons handed over to the Belgian Army were rechambered to accommodate the standard Belgian 7.65 × 53mm rifle cartridge.

A more unusual calibre alteration came from Australia in 1941–42. With a Japanese invasion anticipated, any weapons likely to be useful for home defence were considered and that included trophy sMG08 and leMG08/15s from the world War I. After 1918 many of these were distributed to adorn returned servicemens' clubs. By 1941 many were still there. They were hastily gathered together and the best of them converted to 0.303, mainly by replacing the barrels with modified Vickers Gun barrels, changing the muzzle attachments and introducing a few other modifications. About 2,000 guns were involved in the programme, some 500 of them cannibalized for spares to ensure that at least 1,500 0.303 guns (approximately 1,000 sMG08 and 500 leMG08/15) could be issued to volunteer home defence units.

In addition to these calibre variants, sMG08s captured by US Army units during 1918 were at one point destined for modification to fire the US 0.30-06 rifle cartridge. The war ended before many could be converted and the project lapsed.

The Chinese 7.92mm Type 24, a copy of the German DWM 7.92mm Model 1909.

A Belgian 7.65mm sMG08 being towed in typical pre-1939 fashion by a team of two (replica) dogs.

CHINESE FINALE

The last of the 'German' Maxim Guns to enter production were those made in China during the mid-1930s. China had been an early Maxim purchaser. Their first examples were delivered in 1892 and from then onwards sporadic batches were procured, latterly from DWM. The last batch from DWM included the 7.92mm Model 1909 (essentially the sMG08), still around when Japan invaded the Chinese mainland in 1931. By that time the Chinese Nationalist Army was equipped with a quartermaster's nightmare of weaponry. It made sense to take steps to standardize, so when it came to machine guns it was decided to copy the well-understood Model 1909 direct.

The result was the 7.92mm Type 24, the first examples being delivered during 1935. The production run reached 36,000, including air-cooled aircraft guns. By the end of 1937 Japanese advances and actions caused the production centre (yet to be revealed) to be closed down. Thereafter, the Type 24 was likely to be encountered almost anywhere in Asia, some turning up during the Korean War and in Vietnam.

5 Russian Maxims

The Russian Army and Navy were early customers for the Maxim Gun following demonstrations held in St Petersburg in 1887. At that time, Russian staff officers were enthusiastic proponents of the Gorloff, a local clone of the Gatling Gun, and had little perception of the capabilities of fully automatic machine guns. Maxim's demonstrations changed their attitudes, although initial sales were measured only in tens. Most sales were to the Russian Navy from 1889 onwards, with more following in 1893.

In 1899, the Russian Army made its first significant Maxim Gun purchases, from DWM in Berlin. The initial delivery ran into hundreds, all chambered for the $7.62 \times 54R$ rifle cartridge (R – rimmed), a cartridge still in widespread service to this day. These early guns were placed on field gun pattern carriages, as that seemed, to the Russian military hierarchy at least, the best way to arrange things. The Russo-Japanese War of 1904–05 changed all that, as the bulky carriages attracted enemy fire. Gun crews soon mounted their guns on less obvious types of mounting, such as makeshift tripods or sledges, with which they managed to take a fearful toll of Japanese lives. It was later claimed that Maxim Guns inflicted over half of the Japanese battle casualties suffered during this war.

The Russian Army managed to handle its Maxim Guns well, organizing them into eight-gun batteries, although it was rare for all eight guns to be in action at the same time, for guns were held in reserve for maintenance and cleaning. However, even though the DWM Maxims performed well, they were prone to malfunctions and, by Russian standards, were too easily damaged. Even though Russian gun crews of that period were hand-picked and had to have some measure of education, the guns were expected to suffer rough handling and were thus found wanting.

LOCAL MODELS

In 1905 the Russians introduced their first locally derived Maxim Gun model, the PM1905, built at the Tula Arsenal. At first sight, the gun was much as before, still with many heavy brass or bronze components, including the barrel jacket. The wheeled heavy tripod, a local derivative of a Vickers commercial design, was so arranged that one of the tripod legs could be folded to allow the gun and mounting to be hand-towed on wheels.

The PM1905 production line was not destined to last long, although those completed remained in service for many years. In 1910 a new model appeared, the PM1910 or Stankovy Pulemyot Maksima obrazets 1910g, based on one of the last Vickers Maxim models introduced in 1906. It was this model that was to remain the mainstay of the Russian and Soviet heavy machine-gun arsenal for decades to come.

There were two outstanding features of the PM1910 when compared to the PM1905. Steel equivalents replaced most of the brass or bronze components in an attempt to reduce overall weight and reduce manufacturing costs, but strength remained unchanged – in some areas reinforcement was introduced. To the lay observer the main external change was that the brass barrel jacket was replaced by a corrugated steel jacket that was much lighter (and easier to manufacture), but just as robust. Some of these weight savings were obviated by the introduction of a new carriage design, the so-called Sokolov mounting, named after its designer. This resembled a miniature artillery carriage, complete with heavy wheels, a traversing table and even an armoured shield. It was very sturdy and could be dragged over rough terrain for considerable distances. Once in action the wheels could be removed for the gun to be supported on two forward-folding legs and the U-shaped trail that doubled as a towing handle.

In fact, everything about the PM1910 reflected great strength. The Russian high command knew that the poor education levels of the troops who would handle them would result in harsh treatment and little care or maintenance. The overall result was that the planned weight-reduction programme resulted in a gun that weighed about 24kg (53lb) and a mounting that weighed over 45kg (99lb). Removing the shield reduced the weight slightly, but even a shieldless gun remained a considerable load.

The PM1910	
Model	PM1910
Calibre	7.62mm (0.30in)
Length	1,107mm (43.6in)
Weight	45.2kg (99.7lb)
Muzzle velocity	863m/s (2,822ft/sec)
Rate of fire	520–600rds/min
Feed	250-round belt

MASS PRODUCTION

The weight factor never seems to have bothered Tsarist soldiers or their later Soviet counterparts. The PM1910 was to remain in production for over four decades. By the time production ceased well over 600,000 had been manufactured, making the PM1910 the most numerous of all the many Maxim Gun models. The last PM1910 remained much the same as the first, for, apart from a few minor changes and omissions introduced to meet the prolific production demands of the Great

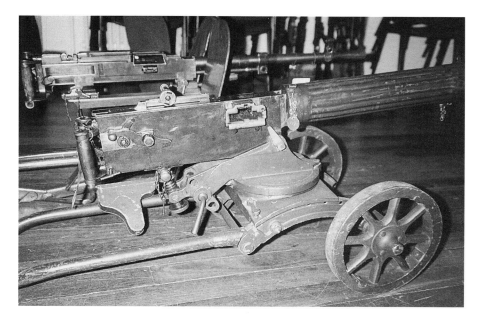

A 7.62mm PM1910 indicating the strength and weight of the Sokolov mounting.

Patriotic War of 1941–45, the PM1910 was altered but little.

This was a deliberate policy dictated by the sheer numbers of the Russian/Soviet armed forces. Soldiers in Tsarist or Soviet uniforms could be counted in millions. To them were added reserve troops, militias, paramilitaries, and so on. They all had to be equipped, trained and supplied in a standard manner, so that meant standard weapons. That, in turn, meant as few changes as possible were made once any weapon had been selected for service – the emphasis then was on mass production in tens and hundreds of thousands, dwarfing most production programmes carried out elsewhere.

At times, such as immediately after the German invasion of 1941, as many refinements as could be managed were omitted, such as side-wind correction devices on the sights. Also after 1941 few considerations were given to cosmetic finish, so many Great Patriotic War period PM1910s had a very rough appearance, even before hard service. But nothing was spared regarding the essential internal operating mechanisms that continued to be manufactured to the usual high tolerances.

As numbers of PM1910s became available from 1910 onwards, so did the variety of uses to which they were put. The usual duties of defending fortifications and various roles at sea soon followed. When the first Russian armoured cars appeared they were armed with the PM1910. The cavalry carried its PM1910s on horse-drawn carts known as *Tachankas*, while many infantry units also carried their weapons on small carts.

GREAT PATRIOTIC WAR

Some development of the PM1910 continued after 1917. To assist production, the forward-folding mounting legs were omitted and from then on the guns were fired direct from their wheels. An air-cooled variant of the PM1910, the PV-1, appeared in 1923, intended for fixed installations on aircraft. It went into production in 1926 and remained there until 1940, although, by comparison with the land-service models, relatively few were made. Cooling also featured on what was perhaps the last PM1910 innovation. Introduced in 1943, this was a tractor fuel cap over the barrel cooling jacket, that not only made refilling easier but enabled snow or ice to be packed in when water was short. The idea was copied from the Finns after the Russians had noticed it during their 1939–40 Winter War against Finland.

Between the wars the Maxim underwent its final development in Soviet hands. Tsarist designers had not managed to come up with a light machine gun during the World War I years, although by the 1920s the Soviets were beginning to do so (*see* Chapter 13). With the Maxim Gun action to hand and well understood, it was decided to adapt it for its intended new role.

The results were not a success. Two models appeared, both with air-cooled barrels and bipods. One was the Maxim-Kolesnikov (M-K) with a strangely contoured butt stock. The other, and preferred model, was the Maxim-Tokarev (M-T) with a conventional butt stock. Despite some perceived shortcomings, such as being heavier than required, the M-T was produced from 1925 onwards.

Only 2,450 were finished before production ceased in favour of a better weapon (the DP – *see* Chapter 13). By Soviet standards this was a puny total, so any level of standardization was impossible. Instead, M-Ts were sent to Spain to arm Republican forces during the Spanish Civil War of 1936–39. Even the few M-K prototypes ended up at the same destination. A few M-Ts must have been retained in the Soviet Union, for there were reports of them in action during the Winter War against Finland, a period when the Soviet armed forces pressed into service anything capable of automatic fire.

By the end of the 1930s it was planned that PM1910 production would be wound down in favour of the DS1939 (*see* Chapter 17). Unfortunately for the Soviets, that gun soon

Defending the railways, a cargo truck carrying a four-gun Tokarev mounting – the gun in the foreground is a 45mm Model 1932 regimental gun.

demonstrated so many faults it had to be withdrawn. The PM1910 was once again given production priority, just as the Germans invaded the Soviet Union. The change of emphasis was marked by PM1910 output rising from 9,691 in 1941 to 55,258 during 1942.

NEW ROLES

In 1931 the PM1910 assumed a new role as a low-level air defence weapon, although its first rudimentary air defence mountings had been devised as early as 1914. For the new role, four PM1910s were mounted side by side on a frame mounted on a high, heavy-duty tripod. The complete assembly was known as the Tokarev mounting. Each gun had its own separate ammunition supply box while a water pump and interconnecting pipes were provided for barrel cooling. All four guns were aimed and fired simultaneously by one crew member while others attended to ammunition supply.

The Tokarev mounting gained a fearsome reputation against low-flying German aircraft and land targets from 1941 onwards, so much so that the

German invaders adopted whatever guns they could capture. The same fate awaited the huge numbers of PM1910s captured by them. The Germans were familiar with the PM1910 as early as 1915, for from then onwards all guns captured in good condition were converted to fire the German 7.92 × 57mm cartridge and turned against their former owners. After 1941 such conversions were unnecessary for, along with the PM1910s, the Germans also seized enormous quantities of 7.62 × 54R ammunition, enough to keep captured PM1910s firing for years. After this date, the PM1910 became a common sight in German hands throughout much of Europe, forming the reserve standard German Maxim Gun. For logistic-support purposes the Germans gave their captured guns the designation of 7.62mm Maschinengewehr 216(r), the (r) denoting *russisches*, or Russian. Many second-line, garrison and reserve German units based throughout occupied Europe were given the 7.62mm MG216(r) designation in lieu of anything better, retaining this label until the end in 1945.

By 1945 the PM1910 was already being phased out of Soviet service, to be gradually replaced by

An illustration copied from a German service manual for the PM1910.

a lighter and more modern design, the SG43 (*see* Chapter 17). But the PM1910 still had many years to go before it vanished. As they were withdrawn from Soviet use, PM1910s were freely handed out to nations deemed to come within the sphere of Soviet influence, and that ranged from established armed forces to so-called freedom fighters in many troubled corners of the world. The last major conflict in which the PM1910 featured as a front-line weapon (in both North Korean and Communist Chinese hands) was the Korean War of the early 1950s, but numbers were still being encountered in Vietnam and parts of Africa until at least the 1980s. Even now, the PM1910 might still be encountered in irregular hands and it would be a bold person who stated that the type has, even now, entirely passed away.

FINNISH MAXIMS

Mention must be made of the Maxim guns manufactured in Finland. They were one result of the post-1918 War of Independence that freed Finland from the yoke of the old Russian Empire. Numbers of PM1910 guns were captured and inducted into Finnish Army ranks as the 7.62mm Model 09-09. In 1921 a lighter tripod was introduced, resulting in the Model 09-21, although by 1932 even those were getting rather worn. It was therefore decided to manufacture a slightly modified PM1910 to keep sufficient guns in service.

Production was carried out by OY Tikkakoski AB of Jyvakyla, the result being the Model 09-32. Introduced changes involved an increased cyclic fire rate of 800rds/min, the ability to feed metal-link belts, and some alterations to the receiver, but basically the gun remained the PM1910. One later modification was the addition of a 'snow cap' to the water jacket, something later copied for late-production Soviet PM1910s.

The 7.62mm Model 09-32 gun remained in Finnish service until at least the 1970s, many of these weapons modified for the low-level air defence role. The Finnish Army also received ex-German sMG08 Maxims during the war years, later converted to take 7.62 × 54R ammunition.

6　Swiss Maxims

Although there were relatively few of them, the Swiss MG11 Maxims deserve a special mention as being the finest Maxim Guns ever made. Maxims made in Switzerland were manufactured to a Swiss watch-level of precision, finish and fine appearance that will never be excelled in a military world now bedevilled by more prosaic considerations.

Swiss military authorities were early enthusiasts of machine guns. During the nineteenth century, as now, Swiss military strategy was heavily weighted towards home defence, relying on fortification systems to keep any enemy from crossing Swiss borders. Machine guns make ideal weapons for fortifications, enabling a few soldiers behind stout defences to keep hordes at bay. At first, the only machine guns purchased were a few Gatling and Gardner Guns for trials, but by 1888 Maxim had entered the scene.

Knowing that the Swiss Army wanted to have rapid-fire guns capable of firing the unique Swiss 7.5×55mm rifle cartridge, Maxim had to adapt his gun to operate with what was then a relatively small calibre round, still in the final pre-service acceptance stages. Until then, most Maxim Gun sales had been for the 0.45in calibre, so scaling down the mechanism introduced a few challenges. These were soon overcome, however, and seventy-two guns were delivered from the UK between 1891–94. These guns, known locally as the Maschinengewehr 1894 or MG94, differed from most other Maxim Gun models in that they were intended to be portable enough for operations with mountain troops. Weight therefore had to be drastically reduced. The brass water jacket was as slim

as could be devised and other weight savings were introduced where possible. For instance, the fusee recoil spring did not have a cover, unlike nearly all other Maxim Guns. A special backpack frame was devised that not only allowed the gun to be carried by a single intrepid soldier, but could be unfolded to form a quadruped mounting adjustable to suit local conditions. Pack animals were also used to carry these guns, as they were with later Swiss machine-gun models.

The MG94 lasted for years. Once these weapons were no longed favoured by mountain troops, they were usually converted for either fortification or air defence duties. The intended replacement (in practice, more of a supplement) was the MG00, this time from DWM of Germany. As these guns were intended for use by cavalry using horse-drawn carts, there was no great urgency regarding weight so the water jacket reverted to its usual dimensions and a conventional tripod appeared. About sixty MG00s were procured. DWM also featured in another purchase, this time for the MG11. A total of 146 were ordered, but in 1915, with the neutral Swiss cut off from any possible outside military supplies, the Swiss authorities decided to manufacture their own guns, using the DWM MG11 as the model.

MG11

Production of the MG11 commenced at the Waffen Swiss Fabrik (usually known as w + f), Bern, in 1915 and continued until as late as 1946.

A Swiss 7.5mm MG11 in a fortification mounting complete with optical sight.

This 7.5mm MG94 Maxim has been modified for the fortification role and is here seen on a display stand – the muzzle attachment is a device for keeping firing fumes out of the fortification interior.

Over that period a total of 10,269 MG11s were made to exacting Swiss standards and it is to these guns that all the superlatives belong. Of this total, eighty had slot-perforated jackets for the air cooling of what became aircraft guns. Guns were also produced for fortifications, tanks and the cavalry. At some point, 2,000 guns were manufactured for sale to Persia, a rare example of Switzerland exporting any form of military materiel.

Throughout its long service life the MG11 was subject to updating measures. From an early stage optical sights, in both telescopic and dial sight forms, became available. By 1935 the guns had been converted to accept flexible metal ammunition link belts instead of the former fabric belts,

which were, as with all of their kind, prone to stretching or warping and one of the main causes of feeding jams. Other changes included adapting the MG11 for air defence, complete with a special high tripod and an optional shoulder stock. Some air defence arrangements included two MG11s side by side on a common mounting. A revised muzzle recoil booster device was another addition. A spaced armour shield was but one option among a host of beautifully made accessories.

The Swiss Maxim Guns were retained in active service until at least the 1960s and maybe for a little while after. Survivors remaining in museums and collections are outstanding examples of Swiss workmanship.

7 The Vickers Gun

The last Maxim Gun model produced by Vickers Sons & Maxim Limited was the Model 1906 'New Light' Maxim Gun. It was considerably lighter than earlier models, due to changing all brass components to steel, the steel barrel jacket being corrugated to impart added rigidity. In addition, the Model 1906 was the first to have a muzzle recoil booster as standard.

Few Model 1906 guns were manufactured, as the German DWM concern was by then penetrating the machine-gun market with its own Maxim-derived guns. However, the Model 1906 was adopted by the Russians as the basis for their PM1910 (*see* Chapter 5), reversing many of the original weight-reduction measures by making everything that much stronger and heavier.

A NEW GUN

Another factor in the demise of the Maxim Model 1906 was that as early as 1907 Vickers' engineers were busy making significant alterations to the operating mechanism. While retaining the reliability and mechanical operation of the Maxim Gun, internal space and weight changes were achieved by inverting the toggle lock so that it broke upwards. This simple revision reduced the depth of the receiver and the mechanical stresses produced during operation. Construction could therefore be that much lighter. Other changes included a revised trigger arrangement, carrying over the characteristic spade grips of the late Maxim Gun models, and some revisions to the feed mechanism.

By 1908 the Vickers Model 1908 Light Pattern machine gun was ready for demonstrations and created quite a stir when it was announced that the gun itself weighed, at 12.7kg (28lb), about half that of the British Army's Maxim Guns, which weighed in at 25.4kg (56lb). Modest commercial sales followed, the largest customer being Italy with 893 guns (but no tripods, as the Vickers product was considered too expensive). Russia was another customer, taking 268.

ARMY ACCEPTANCE

The most important of the early customers in the long term was the British Army. Its initial purchase, made in 1911, was a batch of twenty-six guns, subsequently used for a series of trials that resulted in requests for small modifications before formal adoption of the Gun, Machine, Mark 1 (usually known as the Vickers or Vickers Gun) in late 1911. All these guns were chambered for the British 0.303in rimmed rifle cartridge that was to remain the 'British' calibre until the Vickers Gun was withdrawn during 1968. Production of the 1911 model commenced soon after adoption, yet by the time the World War I began in August 1914 the number of guns delivered totalled just over 100.

Many more were soon sorely needed. At that time each British Army battalion had two machine guns, usually commanded by a lowly subaltern and largely ignored by battalion headquarters. Training levels were variable although rarely thorough. Few officers knew what to do with their machine guns and fewer still took the trouble to find out. A small cadre of officers appreciated the potential of firepower and the machine gun and made attempts to alter machine-gun policies by a series of publications and internal memoranda. The usual result was that they were regarded as cranks by senior officers and largely treated accordingly. Critics chose to overlook the success of automatic weapons during colonial warfare, deeming such experience as non-applicable to 'real soldiering'.

The firepower advocates did manage one major achievement. In order to get as many bullets as possible flying towards the enemy, each infantry-man was trained to a level where he could fire at least fifteen aimed rounds every minute from his bolt-action rifle. This rapidity astounded the rest of Europe, but if machine guns had been more widely distributed they could have more than exceeded the rifles' firepower performance. A Vickers Gun could churn out a steady cyclic rate of 450rds/min.

CHANGING PRIORITIES

Once combat in France commenced, German machine guns came to dominate infantry and cavalry actions. Despite their rapid-fire rifle training, British troops suffered dreadfully from the effects of German machine-gun fire and cavalry regiments were swept from the field. The lack of machine guns with which to respond brought calls for more and yet more from all sectors of the Western Front.

Production at the main Vickers Gun manufac-turing centres grew in leaps and bounds until the premises at Erith and (by 1916) Crayford in Kent had to be enlarged drastically to accommodate the expanding workforce. It was at this point that the Vickers Gun's main shortcoming, carried over from the Maxim, became painfully apparent. Skilled and experienced workers were needed to manufacture the guns to the necessary degrees of precision and these soon became rare. Tolerances

in the internal mechanisms were tight. Neglecting them inevitably led to operational malfunctions and the inability to switch components between guns.

By immense investments in workplace per-sonnel and resources, the number of Vickers Guns arriving in France gradually increased. At one stage production rates reached 800 a month. Machine Gun Schools were hurriedly established and by late 1914 the nucleus of a dedicated Machine Gun Corps (MGC) was already in being. The MGC would ultimately be a formation fielded in addition to the machine guns that were integral within every battalion. MGC batteries were assigned to divisions and corps as required, but perhaps their greatest contribution to the British war effort came as centres of expertise.

It became apparent that just placing Vickers Guns along the trenches was insufficient to gain the best from them. Tactics, logistics and the ability to maintain the guns in action all required specialized expertise, gained only by dedication, familiarity and thorough training. By specializing in the Vickers Gun, the MGC came to learn of its needs and idiosyncrasies, and this knowledge was duly passed down through the command and training chains. Gradually, the Vickers Gun came to dominate the Western Front (and elsewhere) to the degree formerly attained by German machine gunners.

By the time the Great War ended and contracts had been wound down, the total of Vickers Guns manufactured was about 75,000. Concurrent with this output was an equally substantial stream of items such as spares, accessories and even humble fabric ammunition belts. Manufacture of the Vickers Gun developed into a major part of the British industrial war effort.

The initial rate of issue of two machine guns per battalion had been raised to sixteen by the end of 1915. By the end of 1918 the figure stood at as many as sixty-four, although this included MGC guns and Lewis Guns; the usual number of Vickers Guns within a battalion was eight. Matters were never assisted by a wastage rate that at times

The classic side view of the 0.303 Vickers Gun.

reached over 50 per cent due to enemy action, breakages and other reasons. Further demands were imposed by requirements to arm the expanding aviation services, where air-cooled variants of the Vickers Gun were introduced to arm the first combat aircraft.

By 1918 the Vickers Gun had gained an enviable reputation for reliability and durability. Records abound of guns chugging away for extended periods lasting many hours to deny areas of terrain to the enemy, although credit should also go to the gun crews and their training. Their expertise levels reached the point where refinements such as indirect fire 'off the map' against distant unseen targets, using fire directors, dial (panoramic) sights and clinometers, became normal practice.

A fair portion of Vickers Gun production went to other nations. Allies such as France, Russia, Canada, Australia and New Zealand came into the procurement chain.

US PRODUCTION

To meet rising demand from all quarters, in 1915 an approach was made by Vickers to the Colt's Patent Firearms Manufacturing Company of Hartford, Connecticut. The intention was to establish a production line in the USA in order to partially offset demands on the UK lines. However, although firm orders were placed for 16,000 guns, 10,000 of them for the Russian Army, no US-manufactured 0.303in guns materialized.

Colt's was also supposed to be manufacturing Vickers Guns for the US Army, as the type had been ordered as the Model 1915, chambered for the US 0.30-06 cartridge. Due to the manufacturing complexity of the Vickers Gun, the move to full-scale production was slow. Despite urgent US Army orders for 4,125 Model 1915 guns placed during 1915, by the time the USA entered the war in April 1917 only 125 had been partially completed, so none had even reached the troops.

The Vickers Gun carrier version of the Universal Carrier – note the ammunition stowage in the rear compartment.

The first US soldiers arriving in France received UK-made 0.303 guns on loan from the British Army. They retained them until the Armistice. Fortunately for the US Army the differences between the US Model 1915 and the British Vickers were limited to calibre-related items only.

There was an odd footnote to the US Vickers Gun story. Once the war ended the 0.30-06 Model 1915s were withdrawn from US Army service and stockpiled (or sold to Mexico). In 1940 they were dragged out and sent to the UK to arm the newly formed Home Guard, so some US Vickers Guns did eventually reach the UK. A conversion programme allowed those delivered to take 0.303 ammunition.

INTERWAR YEARS

After 1918, Vickers in the UK was at first kept going by completing wartime contracts. As the British armed forces were wound down, so was the need for Vickers Guns. There were more than enough stockpiled to keep the relatively small (by wartime standards) British Army going for years. Fortunately there was a well-established cadre of Vickers Gun experts who, by passing down their knowledge over the years, were able to maintain a high level of machine-gun expertise within the British Army.

There was even some development devoted to making the Vickers Gun more mobile. Motor cycles with special sidecars had appeared during World War I, but they proved vulnerable and of little use in forward areas. The advent of the tank had demonstrated that weapons could be carried around battlefields while protected by armour, so the concept was extended to the Vickers Gun. Small tracked carriers appeared during the 1920s and 1930s, each mounting a single gun that could be dismounted when necessary, and with space for a crew and some ammunition. Although few were produced between the wars, a series of experimental vehicles eventually led to the Universal Carriers of World War II.

Between 1919 and 1939, much of the British post-1918 stockpile dwindled away through a process of handouts to various Commonwealth nations, while Vickers was still able to deliver commercial sales batches of Vickers Guns to many other states. Those nations covered just about every part of the world, apart from the Soviet Union.

Many of the sales during the interwar years related to air-cooled models eventually produced in a series of twelve types. Originally developed for either fixed or flexible aircraft installations, these twelve types included various drum- or belt-feed systems according to the model. They were usually designated by type, or Class, using a letter, such as Vickers Class D or Class F. There were variations within each Class to suit particular

Canadian troops crewing a Universal Carrier with a Vickers Gun. The Vickers Gun is the last production version with an enlarged muzzle booster device and a canvas sleeve for the cooling jacket.

installations. Two, the Class K and Class M guns, were derivatives of the Vickers-Berthier light machine gun (*see* Chapter 13), so were not 'pure' Vickers Guns. By the mid-1930s most of the Vickers air-cooled guns had been withdrawn from service as aircraft guns, only to reappear during the war years on a variety of vehicle or improvised air-defence mountings.

0.50 GUNS

The Vickers Gun also found a place on tanks and armoured cars. For this application water-cooling was retained. The main change from the tripod-mounted guns was the provision of a pistol grip and trigger. Both 0.303 and 0.50in guns were developed, the 0.50 guns being scaled-up versions of the 0.303. A fair proportion of the 0.303 tank guns were conversions from stockpiled tripod-mounted examples.

The Vickers 0.50in cartridge was special to the 0.50 Vickers tank guns, measuring $12.7 \times 81mm$ (the 81mm being the cartridge case length), while there was another Vickers 0.50 cartridge for the so-called Vickers Class D High-velocity guns that appeared during the 1930s. For this application the cartridge was lengthened to 12.7×120 SR (SR – Semi Rimmed) but, although powerful, it proved to be a ballistic dead end as, due to their high unit cost, relatively few of the Vickers High-velocity guns were made or sold.

An aircraft version of the 0.303 Vickers Gun – note the cooling jacket perforations for air cooling.

British 0.50 tank guns were in widespread service by 1939, usually as the main armament of the Vickers Light Tank series. For instance, the Vickers Mark V1 had a Vickers 0.303 and 0.50 mounted side by side in the turret, below protective armour sleeves. Both guns could be dismounted to be fired from an add-on bipod. Few lasted until 1945 as by then they had been replaced by Besa guns.

There was also a naval application for the Vickers 0.50. This was as an air defence weapon on naval vessels, usually in compact quadruple mounts to provide a collective rate of fire of 2,400 rds/min; there was also a dual mounting. These mountings proved quite successful, so much so that naval 0.50 guns by far outstripped the tank guns numerically. These guns should not be confused with the Royal Navy's Vickers 40mm Pom-Poms. Arranged in batteries of up to eight on a single mounting, 40mm water-cooled guns defended many combat vessels but are outside the remit of this account.

WORLD WAR II

To return to the mainstream 0.303 Vickers Gun, by 1939 the supply situation was once again a cause for concern. So many World War I period guns had been converted, handed out or sold that few were left and most of them were already well worn or unsuitable for returning to service. From

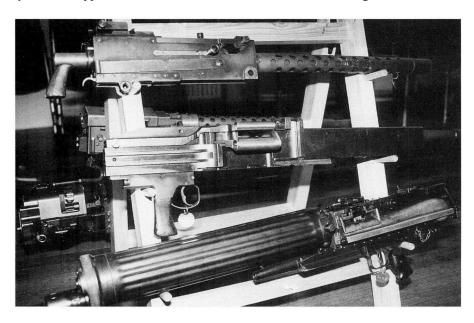

The bottom of this trio of tank machine guns is a 0.50 Vickers Gun. Centre is a 7.92mm Besa, while a Browning M1919 is top.

A Vickers Light Tank Mk IVB armed with 0.50 and 0.303 Vickers Guns.

1939 onwards, many of the older guns were rebuilt or simply cannibalized for spare parts.

Production of the Vickers Gun recommenced at Crayford during 1939, with another back-up facility later being established at Bath, Somerset, as Crayford in Kent was well within range of Luftwaffe bombers. Another production facility had been established in 1929 at Lithgow, in New South Wales, Australia, to supply both tripod- and tank-mounted guns to the Australian and New Zealand armies. Production totals during the war years were 10,170 tripod guns and 284 tank guns. Canada produced barrels and some other spares. UK production stood at 11,828 by 1945.

The manufacturing processes remained much as before, demanding labour-intensive hand fitting and finishing, the only external change being that the barrel water jacket exteriors became smooth rather than corrugated. Jacket strength was maintained by using slightly thicker steel, making the gun marginally heavier than before.

By 1945 the standard of machine gunnery had reached the point where it transcended the usual direct-fire role of the Vickers Gun to that of ultra-long-range area coverage against distant and unseen targets. This was an extension of the World War I indirect-fire techniques, made possible by the introduction of the 0.303 Mark 8Z round. With this round, the bullet had a revised base profile that created less drag during flight and was thus able to travel to greater ranges. In fact, the Mark 8Z round added a further 914m (1,000yd), providing maximum ranges of well over 3,655m (4,000yd). The World War I indirect-fire techniques were further developed to make full use of this extended range potential to the extent that the infantry found itself using complex fire-control procedures and instruments not far removed from those of field artillery. The utility of the Vickers Gun was further developed when armour-piercing ammunition became available, capable of defeating light armoured vehicle protection.

By 1945 the Vickers Gun had become categorized as a medium machine gun to differentiate it from the many light and general-purpose machine guns then established.

THE END

After 1945 the Vickers Gun went on much as before, playing its part in the Korean War of the early 1950s and during several Persian Gulf operations during the 1960s. Thereafter the Vickers Guns in British service experienced a gradual process of winding down until, in 1968, they were officially withdrawn from service. A few remained in Royal Marine Commando units, but by 1970 the lighter and handier L7A2 general-purpose machine gun was well established.

The Vickers Gun did linger on elsewhere, the last known user being the Pakistan Army where the Vickers lasted until the 1980s at least. South Africa was another late user. Beleaguered by UN sanctions and guerrilla warfare around the borders, the South Africans' need for automatic weapons during the late 1960s was such that they converted their guns to fire 7.62 × 51mm NATO

A Royal Marine manning a 0.303 Vickers Gun during the mid-1950s, not long before the Vickers Gun began to be phased out of service.

A Sudanese soldier manning a 0.303 Vickers Gun.

ammunition. In the event, these conversions were issued only to Commando local home-defence units before being replaced by more modern weapons.

The Vickers Gun was sold to many nations outside the old British Empire. All around the world both ground and aircraft guns were employed in many guises. Italy has already been mentioned, but few now realize that one of the most prolific proponents of the Vickers Gun was Japan, where some licensed production took place. European users included Denmark, Greece and the Netherlands. In 1966 Israel captured about 100 guns from Egypt. They were converted to fire 7.92 × 57mm ammunition, although they were little used other than as reserve weapons.

The only Vickers Guns now left are in museums or collections. Perhaps the best memorial to them is that the Vickers Gun became widely regarded with what can only be termed affection by its many employers. It was reliable, sturdy and gave good service throughout its long military career.

The Vickers Gun

Model	Vickers Gun
Calibre	0.303in (7.7mm)
Length	1,156mm (45.5in)
Weight	40kg (88.5lb)
Muzzle velocity	744m/s (2,440ft/sec)
Rate of fire	450–500rds/min
Feed	250-round belt

8   Browning

John Moses Browning was born in 1855 in Ogden, Utah. By the time of his death he had grown from a backwoods' gunsmith into one of the giants of the small arms design world. He was not just a designer but a very practical man. He built his own prototypes and tested them himself, in the process ensuring they were suitable for series production when the time came. His products remain in constant demand and his prolific mechanisms and operating principles remain in active use wherever small arms are produced.

Browning was born into a gunmaking business established by his father. By the time he was twenty years old he was making rifles to his own design and inventing a number of patented small arms designs. The Winchester Arms Company of Hartford, Connecticut, took up one of his first designs, starting an association that was to remain constant for many years. Typical of the numerous products that flowed from Browning's inventive genius was a pump-action small-calibre rifle, still used in fairground shooting booths. The Browning automatic shotgun of 1900 is still a firm favourite. Thanks to the passage of years and the use of numerous manufacturers' names, the origins of many firearms (such as the famous Winchester lever-action repeater rifles and the Colt M1911 pistol) have lost any immediate association with their Browning origins, but he was behind many small arms innovations.

According to legend, Browning's association with machine guns began while he was out hunting. He noted the effects of muzzle blast on nearby vegetation and realized that the blast was wasted energy. If that energy could be harnessed it could be used to operate gun mechanisms. To test the theory a hinged trap plate was placed just in front of a lever-action rifle muzzle. A link connected the plate to the rifle's loading lever and a return spring. Firing the rifle operated the loading lever and the return spring moved everything back to its original position. As long as the trigger remained pressed, the rifle would continue to fire.

MODEL 1895

Browning had established his own small arms manufacturing concern as early as 1880. Using its resources he developed his reloading rifle testbed to the point where the muzzle plate was replaced by propellant gas tapped off from inside the barrel to push an actuating piston and rods to operate the loading and reloading mechanisms. This became known as gas operation, as opposed to the recoil operation of the Maxim and Vickers Guns. By 1890 enough progress had been made for an approach to be made to the Colt's Patent Firearms Manufacturing Company of Hartford, Connecticut, for them to market and manufacture Browning's gun.

Colt's was initially less than enthusiastic. Maxim had already come to dominate the machine-gun markets, while Colt's had suffered from a paucity of sales for the Gatling Gun, in which the company had devoted considerable resources and money. Objections were overcome by a series of firing demonstrations, after which Colt's took to the Browning design with a will.

Last of the Browning Model 1895 line, a 0.30 Marlin Tank machine gun as delivered to the UK in 1940.

Colt-manufactured guns were demonstrated to the US Navy, which purchased fifty as the Colt 6mm Model 1905. An order for a further 150 followed during 1898. As usual, the US Army was not interested, being satisfied with the Gatling Gun.

The Model 1895 was given the nickname of 'Potato Digger', thanks to the gas-actuated linkage arm that swung down under the weapon as it operated. If the arm struck the ground during firing it promptly attempted to dig a hole, hence the name. Despite this odd tendency the Model 1895 was a marked success, sales being made to Austria, Canada, Mexico and Russia. It was light and, thanks to its thick air-cooled barrel, it could keep firing at a steady 400rds/min for long periods (although it could not match the prolonged fire properties of the Maxim Guns). The M1895 also demonstrated the reliability for which Browning machine guns were to become famous.

To complete the story of the Model 1895, the US Army did carry out trials from time to time, and various state militias and other agencies procured small numbers. It was not until 1917 when, with its machine-gun armouries depleted and obsolete, the Army placed an order for about 1,500 guns. This time the Model 1895 was chambered for the 0.30-06 cartridge, and used only for training.

MARLINS

By the time the 1917 and 1918 orders were manufactured, they were a responsibility of the Marlin-Rockwell Corporation of New Haven, Connecticut. The main Model 1915 innovations were the addition of cooling fins to the barrel and a lighter tripod mounting. At the behest of the US Navy, further design development by Marlin-Rockwell did away with the swinging actuator in favour of a piston and rod design.

The advantages of this improvement were such that the US Army seized upon it as a machine gun to arm aircraft. It did not take long to increase the rate of fire for the new role and make the gun suitable for operation with propeller synchronization firing systems so, as the Model 1917, usually known as the Marlin, the revised gun was given a high-priority production status. By the end of 1918, 38,000 Marlin guns had been manufactured, although only a few reached France. A tank gun, the Model 1918, also appeared, the first of them being Model 1917 aircraft guns modified to accommodate a large finned heat radiator sleeve around the barrel.

The Armistice brought an abrupt halt to all Marlin production. Those manufactured were stockpiled, many unused, only for them to be officially declared obsolete in 1932. Most records mention that the remaining stocks of M1917 and M1918 Marlin guns were scrapped. Such a programme may have commenced, but enough were still around in 1940 for 18,240 to be sent to the UK to arm part of the Home Guard. More were placed on improvised mountings to fulfil air defence duties on merchant ships and fishing boats.

BACK TO RECOIL

Almost as soon as the Model 1895 had been type-classified, Browning realized that good as his gas-operation system was, recoil-actuated systems promised greater mechanical efficiency. They also offered better prospects for reduced weight and the ability to operate with many types of ammunition. The problem was that Maxim apparently owned all the patents existing for recoil-operated machine-gun systems. Browning therefore devised his own operating solution.

He devised what is now known as the short-recoil system. At the instant of firing, the barrel and breech block are locked together. Both are then driven for a short distance to the rear by the recoil forces. A cam then disconnects the barrel and breech block, the barrel returning to the original firing position after a short delay. Once the breech block is clear of the breech it comes under the influence of a lever arm known as an accelerator. The latter is a curved lever cam with its pivot located at one end so that any slight movement of the pivot end results in an appreciably greater distance of rapid travel at the other extreme. A combination of accelerator leverage and breech block mass combines to thrust the block to the rear, compressing a return spring in the process. Further rearwards travel is then arrested by a buffer assembly and the return-spring drives everything back to its original position, with the barrel breech and breech block locking together once again. During the rearward travel the spent cartridge case is extracted and ejected, ready for a new round to be loaded into the breech during the forward, return movement. This cycle is repeated for as long as the trigger remains pressed or until the ammunition runs out. The short-recoil system has been retained for all subsequent Browning machine guns.

Browning had devised his recoil-operated machine gun as early as 1901, and the gun was soon at the pre-production phase. Browning included many practical details to make his gun both operable and maintainable by soldiers lacking in technical experience or aptitude. The gun was water-cooled, belt-fed and fired from a tripod. Browning offered his 1901 design to the US Government and, as usual at that time, it was rejected. The Gatling Gun still cast its long shadow and funds were short.

The 1901 drawings were therefore filed against some future requirement. At the time, Browning was not too upset as he was earning a good income from his many pistols and other products and had transferred some of his design skills to Fabrique Nationale (FN) of Liège, Belgium. FN commenced a licence association with Browning in 1897, selling one million Browning pistols by 1912.

M1917

The 1901 drawings stayed in the files until early 1917. By then, the US Army was in a state of semi-uproar. Starved of funds and neglected for many years, the Army found itself preparing to be actively involved in World War I, while having few combat-ready personnel and not enough weapons to arm them, including machine guns. Forecasts were made that over 100,000 machine guns would eventually be needed to equip the new US Army divisions scheduled to be sent to France. All that were to hand were about 1,100 worn-out or obsolete guns. To add to this dearth, there were few ideas regarding which machine-gun models or types should be adopted.

Browning decided his moment had arrived. Knowing that live firing demonstrations were the best weapon-selling tools available, Browning laid on a demonstration to a picked audience in February 1917. That demonstration, held at Capitol Heights, just outside Washington DC, marked a turning point for future machine-gun developments in the USA. The assembled throng of Congressmen, journalists and senior military executives were shown the capabilities of an all-American machine gun. It was the Browning 1901 model with a few modifications, such as an

American classic, the Browning 0.30 Model 1917.

increased rate of fire and downwards spent-case ejection. (Also demonstrated was the Browning Automatic Rifle, but more of that in Chapter 11.)

The response was positive and enthusiastic, although the US military still needed further persuasion. Further tests and demonstrations at the Springfield Armory overcame any remaining misgivings, so the Browning gun was type-classi-fied as the Model 1917 (later more widely known as the M1917) and chambered for the US 0.30-06 rifle cartridge. To ensure that sufficient guns were manufactured in as short a space of time as possible, large contracts were issued to Colt's, Remington and Westinghouse. In the event, the already over-extended Colt concern concentrated on the technical drawings, special tools and gauges to supply to the other two M1917 contrac-tors. Between them, Remington and Westinghouse were able to produce 56,000 guns by the end of 1918, the limited output from Colt adding another 600. To these could be added a further 580 exam-ples with air-cooled barrels for tank and aircraft

Canadian soldiers manning a Browning 0.30 M1917 somewhere on Canada's East Coast in 1940.

installations. This was a prodigious total, considering that production did not really begin until April 1918.

It was September 1918 before the first M1917s reached France, so only a handful saw any combat action before the Armistice intervened.

ANOTHER WAR

As soon as the Armistice was signed the growth in US armed forces strength reverted back to 1917 levels. With that process came a cessation of any further M1917 requirements, so the rapidly established production lines equally rapidly closed down. Many completed guns were stockpiled even before final delivery. During the interwar years some sales of a commercial Model 1928 were made to various South American and other nations, but in general any further development of the water-cooled M1917 lapsed. The M1917A1 did appear during 1935, but that involved just the replacement of the receiver bottom plate, all existing guns eventually being brought up to M1917A1 standard. By the time the World War II began the M1917A1 was still the standard US medium machine gun.

When the USA entered World War II in late 1941, machine-gun holdings were again in a parlous state. Many guns had been disposed of during the interwar years, more had been sold,

The M1917A1	
Model	M1917A1
Calibre	0.30in (7.62mm)
Length	981mm (38.6in)
Weight	38.5kg (85.75lb)
Muzzle velocity	854m/s (2,800ft/sec)
Rate of fire	450–600rds/min
Feed	250-round belt

and 10,000 M1917A1s had been sent to the UK for issue to the Home Guard from 1940 onwards. Such were the demands for machine guns that once again the M1917A1 was placed back into production, not only to equip US forces but for issue to numerous Allied nations, the latter including China for whom the guns were chambered for 7.92mm ammunition. To save scarce raw materials, the bronze water jacket was changed to steel and a few minor modifications were embodied. By the end of 1945, 53,854 M1917A1 guns had been manufactured at several centres.

The M1917A1 remained in service until after the Korean War of the early 1950s. It was replaced only when the 7.62 × 51mm NATO rifle cartridge succeeded the old 0.30-06. No doubt M1917A1s remain in odd corners of the world, although there cannot be many still extant in military hands.

AIR COOLING

Air-cooled Browning machine guns began with a variant of the M1917 for installation on tanks or aircraft, the latter being a secondary role as at that time the Marlin was preferred. For the new role the Browning was provided with a shortened barrel held within a perforated tubular casing. A ball mounting was added, with provision for a small ground tripod for dismounted operations. Optical sights were provided. This became the base Model 1919 (M1919) tank gun, with about 2,500 converted to the role by modifying water-

An export variant of the Browning M1917 was this 7.92mm example delivered to Poland in 1936.

Another Browning classic, the air-cooled 0.30 M1919A4 on its standard tripod.

cooled M1917 guns accordingly. Almost as soon as the conversion programme began, the planned mass production of the tanks and aircraft that the gun was meant to arm was terminated by the Armistice. The stock of M1919 tank guns was used on US Army armoured vehicles until well into the 1930s, with updates being incorporated whenever funds became available.

The first two of these updates were for ground use on tripods. Neither the M1919A1 or M1919A2 proved to be much of a success. An M1919A3 fared little better. It emerged that adding a heavier, lengthened (610mm (24in) as opposed to 457mm (18in)) barrel – back to the same length as the original water-cooled M1917

One of the last variants of the Browning M1919A4 was this 0.30 L3A3 mounted on a Centurion AVRE 165 combat engineering vehicle.

Passing on the knowledge, an American instructor revealing the mysteries of the M1919A4 to British tank troops.

barrel – resulted in a much more satisfactory gun. It was type-classified during the early 1930s as the M1919A4.

The M1919A4 proved to be a winner, used for just about every role that a machine gun could be expected to encounter. It was employed as an infantry weapon on an M2 tripod, as a vehicle pintle or rail gun, for tanks in both coaxial and turret-top forms, for light naval vessels, and so on. An M1919A5, without sights, was developed specifically for cramped tank turret interiors. In typical Browning gun fashion,

guns could be easily reconfigured from role to role with a minimum of effort. Post-1945 M1919A5 variants included the M37 and M37C, the M37 being mainly employed on helicopters and the coaxial M37C on M48 and M60 series tanks.

Both the M1919A4 and M1919A5 remain in widespread service around the world. Some nations, such as Canada and South Africa, have taken the trouble to convert their M1919A4 holdings to accommodate 7.62 × 51mm NATO ammunition, thus elongating their service lives.

The most common of all the Browning air-cooled guns were those produced for aircraft installations, this being a British 0.303 Mark II.

A distinct rarity outside South Africa, a conversion of the M1919A4 known as the MG4 and chambered for 7.62 × 51mm NATO ammunition.

The M1919A4	
Model	M1919A4
Calibre	0.30in (7.62mm)
Length	1.041mm (41in)
Weight	13.95kg (31lb)
Muzzle velocity	854m/s (2,800ft/sec)
Rate of fire	400–500rds/min
Feed	250-round belt

The meticulous records of the US Ordnance Department show that by 1945 no less than 438,971 0.30 M1919A4 machine guns had been manufactured. (The total for all patterns of 0.30 Browning guns manufactured in the USA was 729,430.) That total supplied not just Allied and US armed forces, for many were freely distributed to friendly nations. So many were handed out that they swamped the post-war commercial machine-gun market.

There was one further model that squeezed the last juice from the land service 0.30 M1919 lemon, and that was the M1919A6. After noting the advantages of squad-level light machine guns, such as the British Bren or German MG34, it was decided to adapt the M1919A4 for the role. The result looked most unusual for it included an oddly contoured add-on shoulder stock, a bipod, a special light barrel with a muzzle-flash hider and, on some guns, a carrying handle.

The M1919A6 not only looked odd but was awkward to handle, being still belt-fed and, at 14.6kg (32.2lb), too heavy. These dubious factors notwithstanding, 43,479 M1919A6s were manufactured and widely issued since the US Army had no other easy alternative (other than to purchase from abroad and the international supply situation precluded that). After 1945, US M1919A6 holdings were reduced drastically as they were passed to nations within the American sphere of influence, although it was still a US Army weapon during the Korean War. The M1919A6 was still around in South-East Asia as late as the 1980s.

AIRCRAFT GUNS

The first 0.30 Browning machine gun designed specifically for aircraft use was a rebuilt M1917 with an air-cooled barrel. For various reasons, not the least being the run-down of US squadrons after 1918, numbers were limited to about 3,000 M1918 and M1919 aircraft guns. A Colt-developed gun specifically for the aircraft role appeared in 1922, for both fixed and flexible mountings. Although it looked similar to the ground-based 0.30 Brownings, and used the same operating principles, none of the parts were interchangeable, the numerous differences being introduced to improve reliability once airborne, and the need to feed ammunition from either the left or right according to the installation.

It was 1932 before the gun was ordered by the US Army Air Force and Navy as the AN-M2, the AN denoting Army/Navy as both services used the same model. The AN-M2 went on to be the standard US aircraft gun for many years until, by the early 1950s, it had been almost entirely replaced by heavier calibre aircraft guns. Total US 0.30 AN-M2 production has been recorded as 193,556.

The British also adopted the airborne Browning. In 1926 Armstrong Whitworth (later sublimated into Vickers-Armstrong) acquired a licence from Colt's to produce Browning guns. They set about converting 0.30-06 guns to fire the British 0.303 round, although it was not until1934 that trials were completed and some modifications requested, the main one being that the rate of fire was to be increased from 800 to 1,100rds/min. By that stage the original licensing agreement had expired. After a great deal of discussion it was decided that the British Air Ministry would take over the manufacturing rights for the Browning gun, plus rights to carry out further development. From this, the bulk of the future 0.303 guns would be manufactured by Birmingham Small Arms (BSA) at their Small Heath, Birmingham, facility with Vickers Armstrong and numerous subcontractors playing support roles.

From then onwards the 0.303 Browning machine gun became the main airborne machine gun of the British services. The transition from 0.30-06 to 0.303 was not easy as the 0.303 ammunition used cordite as the propellant, and this could detonate violently if left in a hot barrel chamber. The 0.30-06 rounds, in common with all other ammunition manufacturers other than the British, used a nitro-cellulose propellant with less volatile characteristics. The problems were eventually overcome by ensuring that guns had their breech blocks held to the rear after firing bursts. Another transition challenge was that 0.303 ammunition was rimmed, creating ammunition feed difficulties (0.30-06 was rimless). That challenge was also overcome.

These changes, and the need for British technicians to work to their own drawings, eventually meant the US 0.30 and British 0.303 Browning guns had little in common with each other, apart from visual appearances. By mid-1939 the BSA guns had been finally placed into mass production, just in time for the Battle of Britain in the late summer of 1940, when the eight-gun installations of Spitfires and Hurricanes played their all-important part.

The time span of the eight-gun fighter installations was destined to be short. Despite new armour-piercing and incendiary ammunition being introduced, it became apparent that heavier aircraft weapons would be needed against the increasingly armoured opposition, so the 0.303 fixed guns were phased out accordingly. Flexible and turret-mounted 0.303 guns on bombers and coastal defence aircraft served until well after 1945, but eventually they too were replaced.

By the time BSA had completed its 0.303 Browning gun production run, a total of 468,098 guns had been manufactured, with a peak monthly output of about 16,500 in early 1942. This total does not include Lease-Lend guns sent over from the USA earlier in the war; nor does it include BSA spare-part production, later estimated to be enough for a further 100,000 guns.

OTHERS

So many Browning 0.30 and 0.303 aircraft guns were made that when they became obsolete most were little worn or even unused. Many British and US guns were simply stored away, only to be scrapped later, but many nations could not afford to discard what were still valuable assets. One nation that found an alternative use was Sweden. The Swedish Air Force obtained Colt 0.30 Brownings during the 1930s. They were fixed aircraft guns, soon set aside in favour of more potent aircraft weapons. By 1942 neutral Sweden was short of all manner of weaponry so the aircraft guns were converted to land service weapons for the infantry in much the same manner as the M1919A4 became the M1919A6. The Swedish conversion involved a distinctive bipod made up from two tubular steel loops. A rudimentary shoulder stock was added along with a muzzle-flash hider, sights and a carrying handle. The result was the Kulspruta m/42B. This makeshift was retained for many years, with later conversion to fire locally available 6.5mm or 8mm ammunition. A Browning-based coaxial tank gun, the Kulspruta m/39, is still (2002) in service with the Swedish Army, mounted on vehicles such as the CV90 IFV.

Sweden also had water-cooled Brownings for land service. As far as can be determined these were again the result of a commercial agreement with Colt's. The model, the Kulspruta m/36, was an updated M1917 with revised sights, spade grips, a heavy cradle and an even heavier tripod dating from 1914 – the complete equipment weighed 51kg (112.5lb). It was another long-serving weapon, with diversions to air defence, fortifications and, on dual pintle mountings, armoured vehicles. Three different calibres could be encountered for this weapon, 6.5mm, 7.62mm and 8mm.

Fabrique Nationale (FN) of Liège, Belgium, took out a licence to manufacture Browning machine guns in 1932, producing air-cooled, flex-ible-mounting aircraft guns in several calibres until the war years interrupted proceedings. Limited production began again after 1945, but by then the market was swamped by war-surplus weaponry. FN also manufactured variants of the water-cooled M1917 for commercial sales to South American nations.

M2 BEGINNERS

The year 1918 marked the origins of what was to become the most durable, widely used and best known of all Browning's machine guns, namely the 0.50/12.7mm M2 HB heavy machine gun.

When US Army staff officers first arrived in France in 1918 they carried out analyses of what would be needed regarding future tactics and weapons. Among the latter was a heavy machine gun capable of firing armour-piercing projectiles against tanks, aircraft and armour-protected soldiers. As usual, Browning was ahead of the market. During 1917 he had already started work on a heavier calibre version of his 0.30 M1917 water-cooled machine gun, the short-recoil mech-anism unchanged apart from the all-round scaling increases. He passed the responsibility for ammu-nition design to the Winchester Repeating Arms Company, the objective being a calibre of 0.50/12.7mm to keep the size and weight of the resultant weapon within the bounds of practicality.

Browning's gun design worked. Early experi-ence of excessive judder when firing was over-come by the addition of an adjustable hydraulic buffer assembly that slowed down the rate of fire, while handling was further improved by the

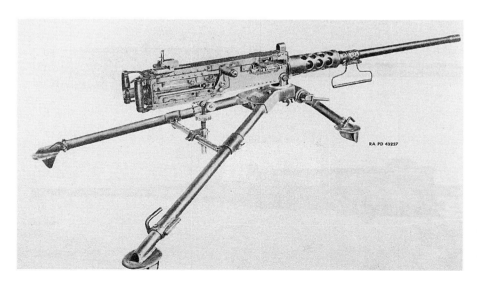

Another Browning classic, the 0.50 M2 HB on its standard tripod.

replacement of the usual Browning pistol grip by spade grips. Unfortunately, Winchester's first attempts at a 0.50/12.7mm cartridge, basically a scaled-up 0.30-06 rifle cartridge, resulted in an under-powered design unable to meet the specifications laid down by the Army. It was hoped that better results would come by installing a longer barrel, but it still looked as though the entire programme would come to nothing.

Salvation arrived with the arrival in the USA of a small batch of captured German 13 × 92mm armour-piercing ammunition intended to be fired from a heavy machine gun, the Tank und Flieger (Tank and Aircraft), or TuF. As it would take time to develop the TuF, the German staff decided to provide their front-line soldiers with a single shot anti-tank rifle (the world's first such weapon) firing the same ammunition. It was this anti-tank rifle ammunition that made its way across the Atlantic. Once examined, Winchester realized its potential and altered the dimensions to suit the 0.50/12.7mm calibre and changed the original case design from rimmed to rimless. The results finally met the desired performance.

However, the heavy machine-gun project remained in trouble. Browning's gun was considered far too heavy by many, and, perhaps more important, by the time the new ammunition was ready it was 1919 and World War I was over. The design languished for over a year, although many soldiers realized the future potential for a 0.50/12.7mm machine gun for air defence. Browning himself regarded his contribution as over, spending more and more of his time with FN in Belgium. It was there that he died suddenly in 1926.

During the 1920s, the Allied nations were awash with weapons left over from World War I, as a result of which US funds for new weapons were almost non-existent. Somehow, Browning's heavy machine gun survived to be type-classified as the M1921 water-cooled ground-mounted gun on a variety of tripods, and the air-cooled M1921 for aircraft. These were little more than test weapons procured in small batches over the years

up to 1934. During that period the gun patents passed to Colt's and it was there, with Browning gone, that much subsequent development work was centred.

In addition to the refinements added by Colt technicians, an ordnance officer, Dr S.G. Green, was so impressed with the potential of the 0.50 Browning that he undertook a drastic revision programme that ensured the gun's future. He developed a basic receiver assembly based on the M1921 guns, but arranged so that it could be easily adapted to no fewer than seven basic gun categories. These included right- or left-hand feed, two models with water-cooled barrels, air-cooled models, aircraft guns and armoured vehicle guns. These receiver/barrel combinations could be swapped around within minutes without recourse to special tools. Other changes included a general strengthening of components so that when more powerful ammunition was introduced, along with a lengthened barrel (1,143mm (45in) as opposed to 915mm (36in)), the mechanism could easily withstand the increased stresses.

Dr Green's efforts resulted in type-classification of the revised gun in 1933. It became the Machine Gun, Caliber 0.50 Browning M2. At the time, this official acceptance had few results as the Great Depression meant no finances for further progress could be expected. The US Army therefore asked the Navy to sponsor further pre-production measures, such as the necessary drawings, spares listings and all the other necessary minutiae needed prior to fielding any new weapon.

Tentative preparations were also made for the M2 to be mass-produced by Colt's and the Springfield Armory.

M2s AT WAR

By the end of the 1930s more defence funding became available and M2 production finally began. By the time of Pearl Harbor, the production total had reached about 300,000, many of which had been passed to the UK and other countries.

During 1942 totals soared, no less than nine manufacturing centres eventually being established. Demand grew so rapidly that short cuts were introduced to speed production.

At first, production was fairly evenly split between water- and air-cooled models (although it should be remembered that the basic types could be switched around at will). The main end-user of the water-cooled models was the US Navy, for the close-in air defence of warships. As early as 1941 it was appreciated that 0.50/12.7mm machine guns had limitations in this role, so the emphasis switched to 20mm cannon and heavier air defence guns. Water-cooled guns, apart from a few relatively static land installations, gradually faded away, to be converted to air-cooled models, especially the M2 HB (HB – Heavy Barrel).

The M2 HB was originally conceived as a cavalry gun but it became recognized as a superlative general-purpose weapon. Gradually more and more M2s were delivered in M2 HB form for just about every machine-gun task that could be conceived. The US Navy continued to use M2 HBs for light craft and the US Army Air Force employed a modified M2 model on almost every one of its combat aircraft, from fighters to heavy bombers. Ground mountings were prolific, from the M2 tripod to numerous vehicle adaptations, from tank turrets to truck hatches. Multiple-gun air defence mountings also appeared. The low-level air defence Maxson Mount originally had two guns, later altered by clever engineering to four. These Maxson Mounts involved M2 HB TT guns, the TT denoting the original purpose for this variant, namely Tank Turret for coaxial, remotely fired installations.

In the air the main model was the AN-M2 with a 36in barrel. Both services, Army and Navy (AN), used the type. In order to produce a faster-firing gun for air warfare the AN-M2 had a rate of fire of 750 to 850rds/min, ground-based guns being 450 to 555rds/min. This was still considered inadequate, so eventually the AN-M3 appeared firing 1,150 to 1,250rds/min. The AN-M3 required a great deal of development time and

resources, resulting in a gun that, while appearing to be identical to the AN-M2 and still retaining the short-recoil principle, was in fact a completely different design with no interchangeability of components between the two. The M3 is still manufactured by FH Herstal of Belgium (the successors to FN) for helicopters, light attack aircraft and air defence, such as the US Avenger missile/gun system.

The importance of the M2 series of heavy machine guns to the Allied war effort can be seen in the combined total of all types by August 1945 – 1,968,596.

M2 TODAY

After 1945 the M2 HB began to fall from favour in some armed forces. The weight of 37.2kg (82lb), just for the gun alone, made it a hefty load to carry by any means. Over the years numerous attempts to reduce the overall weight, by introducing new materials or by careful redesign, have all come to naught. The basic M2 HB has survived by being a reliable, general-purpose weapon for everything from anti-personnel to air defence and vehicle applications. Many armies that at one time phased out their heavy M2 HBs are now re-adopting them, the British Army being but one.

The M2 HB remains in production to this day, FN Herstal of Belgium being one major source. General Dynamics Armament Systems of the USA and Manroy Engineering of the UK are the other two main suppliers. It has been reported that Norinco of China is also offering a M2 HB clone, as well as spare barrels. Several manufacturers continue to offer M2 HB mountings.

One post-war special was the M85 of the late 1950s onwards, intended for use in special traversing roof cupolas on M60 series tank turrets. Among the many changes introduced for the M85 was a dual rate of fire, 350 to 450rds/min for most targets or 1,050rds/min against helicopters. It was also possible to dismount the M85 on to a ground tripod. The M85 turned out to be an expensive

One of the latest, a 0.50 M2 manufactured in the UK by Manroy Engineering, complete with quick-change (CQB) barrel, an optional muzzle-flash hider and reflex ring sights.

proposition and was discontinued when M60 tank production ceased.

There is no sign of the M2 HB fading from the scene. New applications seem to arise every year while new ammunition natures continue to appear, from armour piercing to incendiary. From unpromising beginnings, the M2 HB developed into one of the most successful and reliable heavy machine guns produced to date. It will be a very long time before that accolade fades.

JAPANESE BROWNINGS

As a footnote to this Browning chapter, mention of the Japanese Browning guns should be made. As noted elsewhere, many Browning guns were exported by Colt's during the interwar years, one

The M2 HB

Model	M2 HB
Calibre	12.7mm (0.50in)
Length	1,654mm (65.1in)
Weight	37.8kg (84lb)
Muzzle velocity	884m/s (2,900ft/sec)
Rate of fire	450–575rds/min
Feed	100-round belt

of the keenest customers being Japan. Once examples arrived in Japan they were disassembled and examined closely, prior to unauthorized local production. The most widely deployed result was the 12.7mm Type 1, an aircraft gun firing a locally developed cartridge with a shorter (81mm) case. Closer to the original Brownings were the 7.7mm Type 4 tank gun, the 7.7mm Type 1 aircraft gun and, on a larger scale, the 13.2mm Type 3 aircraft gun. These latter models were not produced in quantity as the Japanese industrial infrastructure became too overloaded – and was being bombed flat as well.

This example of the Browning 0.50 M2 HB was manufactured by FN Herstal of Belgium and features a quick-change barrel (CQB).

9 The Hotchkiss Guns

The early history of the automatic machine gun is littered with the names of Americans who failed to find acceptance in their native country and moved to Europe to further their ambitions. The list contains the name of Benjamin Berkeley Hotchkiss, born in Watertown, Connecticut, in 1826. A talented gunsmith from the time he joined the Colt's Patent Firearms Manufacturing Company, Hotchkiss expanded his design talents into rifled field artillery, impact fuzes and ammunition. By the mid-1860s he was beginning to feel that his efforts were not being adequately rewarded locally so in 1867 he moved to France.

His initial work in France centred on a new type of rifle cartridge soon adopted by the French government. While working in the ammunition field Hotchkiss came to appreciate the potential for a rapid-firing weapon capable of delivering projectiles with explosive payloads, although he was somewhat restricted by the terms of the St Petersburg Convention of 1868 intended to outlaw the use of explosive bullets against personnel. The convention limited the minimum weight of an explosive projectile to 450g, so Hotchkiss designed one weighing 455g. The resultant projectile had a calibre of 37mm, and so a new gun calibre was born.

Hotchkiss then designed a gun to fire his projectile. There is no need to go into great detail regarding the gun as its calibre and manual operation characteristics combine to place it outside the scope of this book. It must be mentioned, however, that the Hotchkiss Gun resembled the Gatling, but with a completely different mechanism. It was a great success commercially,

although only after the French authorities, understandably wary of rapid-firing weapons after their experiences with the unfortunate Mitrailleuse, had extensively tested the gun and its ammunition. They ordered examples for land fortifications and naval applications. There followed a long series of orders from just about every naval power around the world, including the US Navy (and Army), with the guns being manufactured by Hotchkiss & Co., with offices in Paris and London. The main factory was just outside Paris at St Denis, with William Armstrong & Co. manufacturing more guns at its Elswick plant in the UK. It has been recorded that over 10,000 Hotchkiss Guns were manufactured, proof indeed that Hotchkiss had been correct in his advocacy of combining rapid-firing guns and explosive projectiles. A few were still in use in Spain during the Civil War of the late 1930s.

A NEW TEAM

Hotchkiss died in 1885, still inventing novel mechanisms for weapons. His passing left his company in an unfortunate position, for the manually operated rapid-fire gun market was in the process of vanishing. Fortunately for the future of the Hotchkiss company, the technical direction of the concern passed into the hands of another American, Laurence V. Benét, who combined with Henri Mercié to form a strong design team. Another fortunate piece of timing brought an Austrian, Captain Baron Adolph von Odkolek von Augezd, to the Hotchkiss factory with a novel machine-gun design that showed much promise although it was still far from working properly.

In place of the usual royalty arrangement, Benét purchased the rights to the Odkolek design outright and set about refining it to a stage where the weapon stood a chance of acceptance in a crowded market already dominated by Maxim. The first Hotchkiss machine gun, chambered for the French Army's 8mm Lebel rifle cartridge, was ready during 1895 and worked well. One drawback was that, as the barrel was meant to be air cooled, excessive barrel overheating soon became apparent. This was solved by adding five brass 'doughnut' fins around the chamber end of the barrel and making the barrel heavier. The fins radiated excess heat and gave the Hotchkiss machine guns their own distinctive visual trademark.

The 1895 gun used gas operation, propellant gas being tapped from the barrel to (in much-simplified terms) push back a piston and recoil spring to operate the reloading and spent-case ejection operations. Breech locking involved a lug forced out of the bolt to engage in a slot in the side of the receiver as the bolt closed. Only a few components were involved and the gun weight was relatively light at about 9kg (20lb). Ammunition was fed into the gun with the rounds secured in pressed metal strips, each holding thirty rounds. Series of strips could be joined together for prolonged firing. While this feed method did work, it was a constant source of troubles and required special handling skills.

The 8mm Mitrailleuse Hotchkiss mle 1897 was accepted for service by the French Army, who were attracted to the gun's air-cooling features, as many of the French Army's operations at that time took place in the waterless deserts of North Africa. The Hotchkiss guns then went through a series of models. The mle 1898 was an export product (Norway was one customer), while the mle 1900 was almost identical to the mle 1897, other than the original fixed tripod was modified to allow traversing.

ARMY INTERVENTIONS

The number of Hotchkiss guns initially procured by the French Army was relatively limited, the Hotchkiss concern being kept going by export sales, notably to Japan, of which more below. One of the reasons for the French Army's lack of enthusiasm was its belief that its own ordnance engineers at the Puteaux arsenal could do better. In addition, the Army was reluctant to rely on a commercial concern for equipment supplies. At first, Army engineers merely tinkered with the basic Hotchkiss design, eventually unveiling a gun that could fire at a variable rate, from 8rds/min up to 650rds/min, although to what purpose was never explained. That was the mle 1905, but the extra firing-rate control mechanisms proved unreliable and the relatively few examples that the French Army accepted were eventually relegated to fortification duties where their vagaries could be better accommodated.

However, the French Army had not yet finished 'improving' its machine-gun designs. Engineers at the St Etienne arsenal decided on a more drastic design change for the Hotchkiss gun, this time completely reversing the gas-operation principle by having propellant gases driving the piston forward for operations. While this system could work it never worked well or reliably, the resultant guns, the 8mm Mitrailleuse St Etienne mle 1907, being considered as generally unsatisfactory.

The policy of the time was that the mle 1907 would be the standard French Army machine gun, but those delivered all too obviously displayed their worst points when combat began in 1914. They were gradually replaced by Hotchkiss guns, the withdrawn examples either being diverted once again to fortifications or to field artillery batteries for local defence. Despite some drastic modifications introduced during 1915 and 1916, the mle 1907 continued to be less than satisfactory. Those still left after 1918 were sold off to whomever would buy them, or donated wherever French military influence reigned. Yet there were still 11,000 available to the French Army in 1939. A measure of their combat value by then was that the German Army did not deign to divert captured mle 1907 guns for its own purposes.

MLE 1914

When World War I began in August 1914 the French Army, in common with many others, was short of machine guns. The Hotchkiss concern was asked to help to meet the ever-growing demands from the Front, and so it duly supplied its mle 1914. This was basically identical to the earlier models but with the ammunition modified to operate using three-round strips that could be clipped together to form greater lengths. (A mle 1905 employing fabric belt feed was never fully developed.)

Once with the troops, the Hotchkiss mle 1914 proved to be far superior to the unloved mle 1907 and from then onwards the Hotchkiss was distributed throughout the French Army, proving reliable

The Hotchkiss mle 1907

Model	Hotchkiss mle 1907
Calibre	8mm (0.315in)
Length	1,270mm (50in)
Weight	23.6kg (52lb)
Muzzle velocity	725m/s (2,400ft/sec)
Rate of fire	400–600rds/min
Feed	24 or 30-round strips

The St Etienne mle 1907

Model	St Etienne mle 1907
Calibre	8mm (0.315in)
Length	1,180mm (46.5in)
Weight	25.4kg (56.75lb)
Muzzle velocity	700m/s (2,300ft/sec)
Rate of fire	400–600rds/min
Feed	24 or 30-round strips

The standard French machine gun of World War I years and after, the Hotchkiss 8mm mle 1914.

The muzzle attachment on this 8mm St Etienne mle 1907 indicates it is a fortification weapon, as the attachment served to deflect exhaust gases away from the interior of a casemate.

under the worst conditions and relatively easy to maintain. The Germans were happy to turn as many as they could capture against their former owners.

Another non-French user in 1918 was the US Army. The US Army had tested the Hotchkiss mle 1900 soon after it became available, but had decided it offered too few advantages over the already in-service Gatlings. Yet when the first US soldiers arrived in France they lacked any form of machine gun so were supplied with the mle 1914 from French stocks. In all, 9,592 guns were acquired in exchange for raw materials for yet more weapons. This total was enough to equip twelve divisions, leaving about 1,300 guns to be sent to the USA for training. When the war ended the guns in France were handed back to their original suppliers, those in the USA being scrapped as they still fired the 8mm Lebel cartridge, a non-US standard calibre.

Apart from the metal strip feed system, the mle 1914 proved to be reliable enough for the harsh conditions of the trenches, so many being manu-

factured that in 1939 there were still 30,100 left in French armouries. This was despite significant numbers being passed to post-1918 states such as Poland, Yugoslavia and Romania. The mle 1914 saw action during the Spanish Civil War of 1936–39.

The mle 1914 continued to arm Free French and Vichy forces after 1940 and the victorious Germany Army found them useful enough to equip some of their garrison forces in France. By 1945 there were few left as front-line weapons.

JAPAN

The Hotchkiss mle 1900 guns sold to Japan (and licence-produced there) proved their combat worth during the Russo-Japanese War of 1904–05. In typical fashion, Japanese technicians copied the Hotchkiss design and mechanisms to create their own series of Hotchkiss-based machine guns, the first being the 6.5mm Heavy Machine Gun Type 3 introduced during 1914. This still

A Japanese 6.5mm Type 3 heavy machine gun with one of its carrying handles in place.

resembled a Hotchkiss gun but there were more barrel fins. In addition, the adoption of the 6.5mm Arisaka rifle cartridge meant that the easiest way to get around spent-case extraction and other difficulties was to incorporate an oiling mechanism that imparted a thin coating of oil to each round as it was fed into the gun. Needless to say, this oiling feature could cause trouble in dusty or sandy environments, but the Japanese seemed to be happy enough to live with it. Using typical Japanese practicality, holes were provided in the tripod for poles to be inserted to act as lifting handles for the entire gun and tripod as a single team load.

While the 6.5mm Type 3 was still around in 1941 it had been recognized for some time that the low-powered 6.5mm cartridge was inadequate for the machine-gun role. From 1932 onwards it was therefore supplemented by the 7.7mm Type 92. The main changes to the gun were limited to calibre-related components and prominent downward-pointing spade grips – the oiling mechanism was retained. It was the Type 92 that became the main Japanese heavy machine gun between 1941

and 1945, although there was the slightly lighter Type 1 introduced in 1941. To confuse matters, the Type 1 could only fire a marginally different 7.7mm cartridge from the one used for the Type 92. Fortunately for the Japanese supply chain, the more widespread Type 92 could fire both types of ammunition. This was just as well, for by 1945 the Japanese war machine found itself saddled with no fewer than eight cartridge families. Other nations got by with just one or two.

For many years after 1945 the 7.7mm Type 92 served with several Far East armed forces, both regular and irregular, but at over 55kg (121.3lb)

The Type 3	
Model	Type 3
Calibre	6.5mm (0.256in)
Length	1,370mm (45.5in)
Weight	28.1kg (62lb)
Muzzle velocity	742m/s (2,434ft/sec)
Rate of fire	400–500rds/min
Feed	30-round strips

complete it was really too heavy. Some were encountered during the fighting in Vietnam.

THE BIG HOTCHKISS

To return to the French Hotchkiss story, the stock-piled legacy of World War I meant there were few commercial opportunities for new designs during the interwar years. One that did manage to achieve a measure of success was the heavy 13.2mm mle 1930, the long-term successor to an 11mm version of the basic Hotchkiss gun designed in 1917 and intended to be fired against enemy observation balloons. The 1917 attempt proved to be too heavy and fired an under-powered cartridge, so it was not adopted.

The mle 1930 was a brand new design, the only items in common with earlier Hotchkiss guns being a strip feed system and gas operation. However, an alternative overhead box magazine holding thirty rounds was available. The mle 1930 was marketed in three forms, each with its own associated mounting. The three were cavalry, infantry/anti-tank and anti-aircraft. For the anti-

The Hotchkiss mle 1930	
Model	Hotchkiss mle 1930
Calibre	13.2mm (0.519in)
Length	2,413mm (95in)
Weight	37.5kg (87lb)
Muzzle velocity	800m/s
Rate of fire	450rds/min
Feed	30-round box

aircraft role complex dual- or single-gun mountings were available.

With funds short, few mle 1930 guns were adopted by the French Army. Numbers were sold to Poland, Greece, Yugoslavia and Romania, but the batch sizes were never large as the mle 1930 proved to be a complex and expensive proposition.

Perhaps the most avid customer was, again, Japan. The Japanese adopted the mle 1930 as their 13.2mm Type 93, without the strip feed feature and mainly as an air defence gun. It was built at the Kokura arsenal and was issued from 1933 onwards.

A 13.2mm Hotchkiss mle 1930 heavy machine gun in use as a light air defence weapon.

96 Frankreich

Infanterie: Begleitwaffen-Kompanie

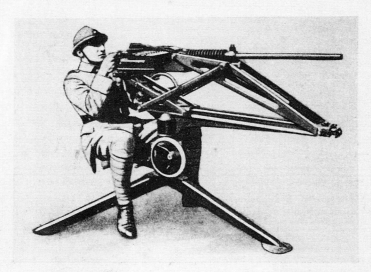

13 mm ss. M.G. (Hotchkiss) M. 30

Technische Angaben: ss. M.G. 13 mm (Hotchkiss) M. 30.

1. Bauart ..... Gasdrucklader
2. Lauf .... angebohrt
3. Laufweite .... 13,2 mm
4. Kühlung .... Luft
5. Patr.-Zuf. ... Magazine zu 30
6. Schießgestell: Dreifuß für 1 oder 2 M.G.
7. Schutzschild .... nein
8. Zusatzgerät f. Fliegerabwehr: Fliegervisier „Le Prieur"

9. Feuergeschw.: 450 Schuß/Min.
10. Größte Schußweite .. 8250 m
11. Gebr. Entfernung:
    direkt .... 3500 m
    indirekt .... — m
12. V° .... 800 m/s
13. Gewicht M.G .... 49 kg
14. Gewicht Schießg. ... 160 kg
15. Gewicht insg. ...... 209 kg

Beförderungsart: Kraftfahrzeug.

An illustration from a German recognition manual depicting a Hotchkiss 13.2mm mle 1930 on an optional ground target or air defence mounting that must have cost as much as the gun itself.

10 Bergmann, Dreyse and Others

The sMG08 and the later leMG08/15 may have dominated the German machine-gun scene, but they were not the only machine guns produced by the Central Powers before 1919. There were several others, although they rarely achieved any significant production totals and so faded from memory, remaining unknown to many. Most of them had some attribute or other but rarely anything that could score significantly over the sMG08. The sMG08 became so well established that it would have taken something really remarkable to be considered as its possible replacement. If this were not so, one rival could have been the Bergmann machine gun.

BERGMANN

Although the name Bergmann is usually employed, Louis Schmeisser (a name later to be closely connected to the history of the submachine gun) probably devised the machine gun first patented in 1900 by the Bergmann Industrie Werke at Suhl. The first Bergmann machine gun was the belt-fed Model 1902, a simple, reliable and compact design chambered for the 7.92 × 57mm cartridge and firing at a rate of 400–450 rds/min. The gun employed a slight variation of the Browning short-recoil principle, although when it was first devised in Germany Browning had yet to get around to converting his short-recoil ideas into hardware, so the assertion that 'great minds think alike' seems apposite.

On firing, the recoil made the Model 1902 barrel and bolt move back together for a short

distance before the breech block was lowered and the bolt was disconnected to be further propelled to the rear by a cam arrangement. This provided sufficient momentum for all the usual return spring compression, ejection, fresh round feeding and locking operations. The receiver was well sealed against the intrusion of debris and, most unusual for the time and especially as the Model 1902 was water-cooled, it was possible to change the barrel within about twenty seconds. Another novelty on the later Model 1910 was the introduction of individual metal links in place of the usual fabric ammunition feed belts.

A Model 1910 and then a Model 1915 appeared, the only major changes being to the mounting. German Army weapon selection personnel were impressed by the Bergmann, especially as it was much lighter and more portable than the sMG08 (at about 13kg (28.7lb) for the gun alone). Their extensive testing also showed that the gun was reliable and easy to maintain. But they still decided to stick with the sMG08.

However, that was not the end of Bergmann machine guns, for in 1915 the 7.92mm MG15nA appeared, the nA denoting *neues Art*, or new model. The main change was that the barrel became air-cooled within a perforated barrel casing, the rest of the mechanism remaining much as before. A side-mounted drum containing a belt of 200 rounds, a rudimentary butt plate and a short tripod were added.

The MG15nA was selected for German Army service, the first being issued during 1916. Most of the output appears to have been sent to the Italian Front to avoid supply complications along

The Bergmann MG15nA

Model	Bergmann MG15nA
Calibre	7.92mm (0.312in)
Length	1,121mm (44.13in)
Weight	12.92kg (28.5lb)
Muzzle velocity	892m/s (2,925ft/sec)
Rate of fire	500rds/min
Feed	200-round belt

the more important Western Front. From the few references remaining regarding the MG15nA, which seems to have been regarded as an expedient interim measure, it appears that the guns were serviceable enough, although the barrels tended to overheat rapidly. When the leMG08/15 became available the Bergmanns were gradually withdrawn.

DREYSE

The name Dreyse was an important one within the realms of German small arms designers, mainly for the Dreyse rifle, the so-called 'Needle Gun' that did much to help to defeat the French Army in 1870. By 1907, when the Dreyse machine gun was first patented, Niklaus von Dreyse had been dead for forty years and his company's assets at Sömmerda in Thuringia had been taken over by

an industrial concern that eventually assumed the Rheinmetall name. Once again, the name of Louis Schmeisser was associated with what had been named the Dreyse machine gun, but the Dreyse mechanism differed from that of the Bergmann.

The 7.92mm Dreyse machine gun did operate along similar lines to the Bergmann, except that the breech block pivoted after firing whereas that for the Bergmann was lowered. This may sound like a mere detail, but the resultant action made the entire gun lighter and more compact. In fact, the Dreyse was the lightest water-cooled machine gun available when the first of them was selected for German service in 1912. That service was limited, for by then it had been decided to concentrate on the sMG08.

A 7.92mm Model 1915 appeared, apparently for service in the Middle East. This was a Model 1910 altered to accommodate a bipod under the water-cooling jacket. The usual spade grips were retained, which must have made handling awkward. Not many appear to have been produced and those few were probably conversions from the standard model.

It was not until 1918 that the updated 7.92mm Model 1918 (MG18) was ordered into mass production. This was not only to boost the numbers of machine guns reaching the fronts, but also in answer to a requirement for a sustained-fire machine gun that was lighter than the sMG08.

The MG18 arrived on the scene too late, as the Armistice intervened. Any further German machine-gun development had to be continued by clandestine means to avoid the terms of the Treaty of Versailles. However, a light model of the Dreyse, complete with an air-cooled barrel, was completed before the war ended. That gun eventually became the MG13, of which more in Chapter 16.

AUSTRIAN DÉBUT

One of the least known of the early machine guns, outside Austro-Hungary at any rate, was devised by a team comprising Grand Duke Salvator and Colonel von Dormus. That was in 1888. Between them, they managed to design what looked a very flimsy and awkward water-cooled weapon operating by what became known as retarded blowback.

Simple blowback depends on the mass of the breech block ensuring the breech remains closed while the bullet is travelling down the barrel. This is safe enough for limited power cartridges, such

as those for light calibre pistols, but regarded as unsafe for the more powerful rifle cartridges with their increased propellant loads. The Austrian pair overcame this by keeping the breech closed by a system of springs and a heavy pendulum that held the breech locked in place until it had pivoted out of the way. By that time, the chamber pressures had fallen to a safe level. As the breech mass was by then moving to the rear there was still enough energy left to carry out the usual loading and reloading procedures. Ammunition was fed into the receiver from an angled overhead single-stack hopper.

The Grand Duke and the Colonel sold their patent rights to the Škodawerke at Pilsen, then one of the major weapon manufacturing concerns of Europe, on a par with the mighty Krupps concern of Germany. Škoda managed to get the Austro-Hungarian Army to adopt what became the Škoda Model 1893 – no doubt a bit of political arm-twisting was involved, for the military appear to have been far from enthusiastic. Despite its low weight of 11.35kg (25lb), the weapon had little

The Skoda Model 1909, complete with a shield for the gun and crew.

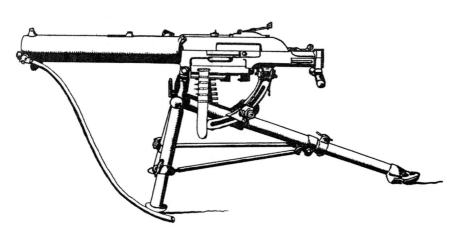

Drawing of a 8mm Schwarzlose 07/12 on a typical heavy tripod.

impact on the ossified Austro-Hungarian military attitudes of the period. Almost all guns produced, chambered for various calibres from 6.5 to 11mm, were deemed suitable only for fortifications. There were no other takers.

Škoda technicians managed to overcome many of the Škoda Model 1893's shortcomings by a drastic redesign programme. From this emerged the Škoda Model 1909, a gun with a more conventional appearance, thanks to its belt feed and the replacement of the spring-loader pendulum by a series of buffers. The Model 1909 was light and serviceable but it got no further than trials before being relegated to small arms history.

SCHWARZLOSE

Andreas Wilhelm Schwarzlose was an inventive German gunsmith from Charlottenburg. He devised several models of semi-automatic pistol before turning his creative attentions towards machine guns in about 1900. His results were not immediately appreciated within Germany as the locals favoured Maxim-derived designs (*see* Chapter 4). He therefore offered his designs to the Steyr rifle works in Austria just around the time when officials of the Austro-Hungarian Army

were investigating machine-gun developments elsewhere. They had purchased Maxim Guns as early as 1889 but preferred a local source of weapons. In 1907, after years of tiresome testing, they adopted the Schwarzlose machine gun as their water-cooled and belt-fed 8mm Maschinengewehr 1907, or MG07.

The Schwarzlose MG07 was unusual in several respects, not the least being that it was simple, not only in operation but also in manufacturing and maintenance terms. It was another machine gun that depended on delayed blowback, but in a different manner than the earlier Škoda equivalent (by 1907 already regarded as obsolete). The MG07 depended on two design innovations. One was a locking system that was never positively locked but which introduced a slight delay before the breech block moved after firing. The other was a relatively short barrel that ensured the bullet was well clear of the muzzle before the breech block began to move to the rear.

The breech-block delay was introduced by the block being linked to an elbow-type linkage and the pressures of a strong spring. Both factors had to be overcome before the breech block was driven to the rear by the recoil forces produced on firing. The short barrel meant that the internal chamber pressures had been reduced to a safe level before

An 8mm Schwarzlose 07/12 heavy machine gun in action in the Austrian Alps.

the breech block moved. As this barrel length was critical (no more than 526mm (20.5in)), it meant that propellant combustion was still incomplete when the bullet left the muzzle, so the resultant severe muzzle flash and blast had to be partially hidden by a long cone-shaped muzzle attachment. This flash hider became a recognition factor for Schwarzlose machine guns.

One of the most important points regarding the Schwarzlose mechanical operations was that the mechanisms were simple and capable of being disassembled within seconds. However, some of this simplicity was offset initially by a necessity to lightly oil each cartridge as it was fed, the resultant lubrication assisting the extraction process after the cartridge case expanded against the chamber walls on firing. Another possible disadvantage was that there seems to have been no incentive to reduce the overall weight. The counter to this was that the substantial nature of all components ensured it could withstand rough and prolonged usage without wearing out. The MG07 alone weighed nearly 20kg (44lb) and the usual tripod almost as much. Its rate of fire was relatively low at around 300rds/min.

A Schwarzlose MG08 was produced for export sales, a major licence production customer being the Netherlands, then usually known as Holland. After 1912 the MG07/12 incorporated a number of modifications, one being the omission of the cartridge oiling system as it was found that the momentum of a heavier breech block could

A 7.9mm Schwarzlose 07/12 machine as delivered to the Dutch armed forces.

overcome any extraction difficulties. There was also an air-cooled MG07/12/R16 intended to arm Austro-Hungarian combat aircraft.

The MG07/12 went on to become by far the most important of the Schwarzlose models, many remaining in service as late as 1945. By then many were in German hands and some had undergone conversions to calibres other than the original Austro-Hungarian 8 × 50R, 7.92 × 57mm being the most common. The Schwarzlose export list included Bulgaria, Greece and Romania. After 1918 more users appeared in Czechoslovakia (later converted to fire 7.92 × 57mm ammunition, with local production lasting until 1931), Hungary, Italy (war reparations), Sweden and Yugoslavia. Examples continued to crop up in odd corners for years after 1945. One known example

surfaced in Albania during the late 1990s, although it seems doubtful it was on the local active list.

PERINO

The first Italian machine gun was designed in 1901, the brainchild of one Giuseppe Perino, who was in charge of the main Italian artillery factory then based in Rome. As so often with Italian engineering efforts, the Perino machine gun was well thought out and bristled with technical innovations that in many respects were far in advance of their time. The Perino design seemed so promising that the Italian military authorities considered it ahead of anything else then on offer. They accordingly decided to keep all details confidential, going to the extent of carrying out trials with overseas machine-gun types to disguise that they were actively considering a home-produced product.

Perino's design featured a most unusual but efficient ammunition feed system. An ammunition feeder to the left of the receiver could be loaded with metal strips, each holding twenty-five rounds of 6.5 × 52mm rifle cartridges. These strips were indexed into the receiver, the rounds being lightly oiled to assist extraction as they were removed

The Schwarzlose sMG07/12	
Model	Schwarzlose sMG07/12
Calibre	8mm (0.315in)
Length	1.066mm (42in)
Weight	39.7kg (87.5lb)
Muzzle velocity	620m/s (2,050ft/sec)
Rate of fire	400rds/min
Feed	250-round belt

from the strip to be chambered and fired. After case extraction the spent case was slotted back into the feeder strip. As strips fed into the receiver more could be added to the top of the ammunition feeder stack.

That was only one Perino innovation. There was also the matter of barrel cooling. Inside the barrel water jacket the barrel was finned to assist cooling, while the fins also doubled as paddles to keep water circulating within the jacket. In addition, water in the jacket could be readily topped up at any time. Further cooling considerations were given to the chamber area, where a small piston-based system circulated cooling air.

The operating mechanism was driven by a long-recoil travel considerably assisted by a muzzle attachment that provided extra recoil power as the bullet left the muzzle. The recoiling barrel drove a system of accelerating levers that thrust the breech block to the rear where it was arrested by a buffer mechanism. As the block was returned to the battery another accelerator lever helped to drive a fresh round into the chamber before it had reached the home position where firing took place. A refinement was that the bolt return speed could be varied at will to alter the cyclic rate of fire up to a maximum of 600 rds/min.

The Perino certainly worked, but it did have its faults. There were too many access points for dust and dirt to find their way into the mechanism and cause jams, with the cartridge-oiling system not helping in this respect. These drawbacks were partially offset by the ability to open the entire right-hand side of the receiver to gain access for jam clearing and other maintenance.

The Italian Army worked on the Perino for years, although only a few development prototypes were actually made for trials that seem never to have been conclusive. When World War I intervened in 1914 the entire design was dropped in favour of another more readily available weapon, the Fiat-Revelli.

FIAT-REVELLI

It is now not possible to determine if there were any direct contacts between Perino and one Bethel Abiel Revelli. Both were based in Rome at around the same time and both were interested in machine-gun mechanisms. Their resultant machine guns had many features in common, such as a side strip feed, a cartridge-oiling mechanism, and not enough attention paid to keeping debris from the interior.

However, the water-cooled gun that Revelli produced in 1908 differed in operation from the Perino. It used a rather harsh delayed blowback system, with the breech block being briefly prevented from parting with the barrel at the firing instant, when chamber pressures were at their highest, by a swinging wedge system. The complicated feed mechanism also differed. An ammunition box on the left of the receiver had ten compartments, each holding five rounds. As each five rounds were consumed the system indexed to the next row of five, and so on.

Not much happened to the Revelli design for some years. The Italian Army was still considering the Perino when the start of hostilities in 1914 changed everything. Machine guns were then needed urgently. The Revelli design was passed to the Fiat automobile concern where some final adjustments were introduced before the gun went into series production. From then on the machine gun was officially known as the 6.5mm Mitriaglice Fiat 14, although the usual title was Fiat-Revelli.

In action, the Fiat-Revelli proved far from satisfactory. The ingress of debris was a constant source of troubles compounded by the need to oil the cartridges to assist extraction. Further debris could be fed into the gun from an externally mounted buffer rod that moved rapidly just in front of the firing grips, forming a constant hazard to the operator's fingers during operation. The ammunition feeder was easily damaged, while the $6.5 \times 52mm$ cartridge soon demonstrated it was not powerful enough for the machine-gun role.

An Italian armoured railway car with a turret mounting two 6.5mm Fiat 14 machine guns.

However, as it was then the only machine gun that the Italian Army could depend on from home sources, large numbers were manufactured, so many in fact that examples were still in service when Italy entered World War II on the wrong side in 1941. The World War I veterans then took part in a second major conflict, although there had been a few changes.

These came in 1935 with the 8mm Mitriaglice Fiat 1914/35. While this had the same basic gun mechanism as before, the modello 1914/35 demonstrated some significant modifications. For a start, a more powerful 8 × 59mm cartridge was introduced, this time fed into the gun in 300-round belts. It was hoped that cartridge oiling could be avoided by the addition of a fluted chamber that reduced the area of the expanded spent case still in contact with the chamber wall after firing. However, primary extraction difficulties remained, so oiling had to be retained.

The most drastic modification was the elimination of water cooling in favour of a heavy

The Fiat 14/35	
Model	Fiat 14/35
Calibre	8mm (0.315in)
Length	1263.5mm (49.75in)
Weight	36.6kg (81.25lb)
Muzzle velocity	790m/s (2,600ft/sec)
Rate of fire	500rds/min
Feed	300-round belt

The water-cooled 6.5mm Mitriaglice Fiat 14.

air-cooled barrel with a quick-change facility. The latter was very necessary, for the barrel rapidly became overheated, restricting burst firing considerably and causing 'cook-offs' when the heat of the chamber inflicted unwanted propellant ignition. In these aspects the modello 1914/35 proved to be less capable than the original model, while the old dirt ingress problems remained.

Many modello 1914/35 guns were converted from water-cooled Fiat-Revelli guns. Newly manufactured guns were known as the modello 35. Neither proved satisfactory in action, but the Italian Army was so short of combat material it had few alternatives. The modello 1914/35 was still around in 1945 when the war ended.

The air-cooled 8mm Fiat 1914/35.

11 Early Portables

Until 1914 the rifle formed the established firepower base for the infantry, with additional fire support provided by field artillery batteries. The advent of the machine gun changed all that by providing masses of firepower from a single infantry-based source, simply by pressing a trigger. Once military hierarchies had grasped that unwelcome fact, urgent demands for more and yet more machine guns arose.

As mentioned in previous chapters, the early machine guns were heavy and bulky sustained-fire weapons that required a crew to serve them. Moving them about was no easy matter, so they tended to be fired from relatively static or prepared positions. This mattered little during trench or fortification warfare, but infantry tacticians came to appreciate that infantry forces carrying out attacks or trench raids could usefully employ the machine gun's firepower. Their early efforts to aquire that extra firepower were negated by the sheer weight and bulk of the Maxim and similar guns that precluded any easy movement, and by a continued tendency to keep machine guns under centralized control. But what the troops were really demanding was portability, and that entailed lighter weights. Those assets had to be paid for by reducing the prolonged and sustained-fire production properties of the machine gun.

This brought about a split in machine-gun development. The water-cooled Maxim pattern weapons became categorized as heavy machine guns. Portable, air-cooled weapons, less capable of sustained fire, became light machine guns.

The light machine gun was in being for years before its true tactical niche became recognized.

Early attempts to make machine guns portable were simply confined to weight reduction, with no great insight into how they would be employed in action. Some sort of application for cavalry forces was usually mentioned in sales literature, but no great thought was given to portable employment by the infantry.

Several light machine guns existed prior to 1914. We will first consider one of the most unusual, the Madsen gun. Many researchers now consider that this gun was the first light machine gun to be manufactured in quantity.

MADSEN

The origins of the Danish Madsen gun are still difficult to determine, for at least two individuals seem to have valid claims to the original design and other names soon became associated with it. The name Madsen was taken from the Danish Minister of War, Captain W.O. Madsen, during the late 1890s when the new design was adopted by the Danish Navy. His enthusiasm for a local product came at a time when the Danish armed forces were actively investigating machine guns. So fervent was Madsen in promoting the Danish product that it received his name, even though he almost certainly had nothing to do with the design.

Two names stand out as the possible designers. One was Julius Alexander Rasmussen, director of the Royal Military Arms arsenal in Copenhagen at the time he applied for a patent in June 1899. However, in February 1902 Lieutenant Theodor Schouboe of the Danish Army patented the same basic operating principles as the Rasmussen design. To add to the confusion, Rasmussen's patent rights were later assigned to the Dansk Rekyriffel Syndikat (DRRS) of Copenhagen where the first hardware was assembled, the same concern later being renamed the Dansk Rekyriffel Syndikat AS 'Madsen' and, eventually, the Dansk Industri Syndikat AS 'Madsen' (DISA). To add to the list of names and general confusion, the Madsen gun was also marketed in some parts of the world under the name of Rexer, while Schouboe later acted as a representative for the Dansk Rekyriffel Syndikat.

Leaving the origins aside, the Madsen gun employed a unique operating principle. In over-simplified terms, at the instant of firing the barrel recoiled to the rear. The breech block carried a stud that was forced back. After about 12.7mm (0.5in) of free travel the stud moved upwards on a fixed switch plate, allowing a combined extractor/ejector to lever the empty cartridge case out of the chamber and down out of the gun. The stud continued along the top of the switch plate, cocking the hammer and compressing a spring. When the stud reached the end of the top surface

of the switch plate the block was forced down by a powerful spring. A pivoted feed arm rotated forward to drive a fresh round out of the magazine and into the chamber. The breech block then followed an alternative track on the switch plate as it was forced forward and upwards to complete the cycle by finally moving forward horizontally and locking.

To say the Madsen mechanism was unusual is something of an understatement – it was unique.

A typical Madsen machine gun without its usual curved box magazine.

A Madsen machine gun, complete with bipod, stock monopod and the usual curved magazine.

All the operations took place within a very compact receiver. Without going into great technical detail, the operation was subject to the point of cartridges becoming slightly distorted as they were fed into the chamber, thereby creating feeding jams, one of the Madsen's most common failings. Yet somehow the Madsen gun worked and was deemed reliable enough to remain in production for over fifty years. It was sold all around the world for just about every rifle calibre then extant (although observers noted that the rimmed cartridges tended to jam more often than the rimless types). Well over 100 models have been listed.

In time, belt-fed versions of the Madsen appeared, as did aircraft guns. All of them were air-cooled, gunners being trained to limit bursts to prevent barrel overheating, something made easier by a relatively slow cyclic rate of fire (about 400–450rds/min) and a box magazine capacity limited to, at best, forty rounds. While the weight varied from model to model, the usual was about or just over 10kg (22lb).

The first Madsen gun sales were to Denmark, Norway and Russia, the cavalry being the main recipients in the Russian Army. The German and US armies both found the Madsen wanting and rejected it from further consideration, although eventually the German Army did become a Madsen user. That followed the Tannenberg and Masurian Lakes battles of 1914, when so much Russian weaponry and equipment fell into German hands that they were happy to absorb much of the spoils into their own armoury.

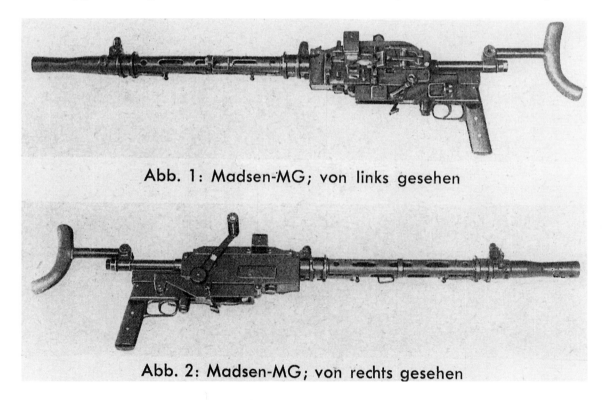

Abb. 1: Madsen-MG; von links gesehen

Abb. 2: Madsen-MG; von rechts gesehen

Two illustrations from a German service manual relating to a belt-fed 7.92mm Madsen machine gun for flexible aircraft installations.

An 8mm Madsen machine gun as delivered to the Danish armed forces for use as a tripod-mounted gun.

The haul included numerous 7.62mm Madsen guns, so many that the German ordnance authorities had to find a use for them. After converting them to the standard German 7.92mm calibre, most were sent to the Western Front where, throughout 1915 and 1916, the guns were issued to specially formed, self-contained Musketen-battalione. These formations were held in reserve at various points behind the front lines to be dashed forward as 'firepower brigade' measures to shore up parts of the line wherever an Allied breakthrough seemed imminent. Madsen guns were considered successful in this role, although the true light machine gun concept had yet to be fully grasped – the Madsen guns were employed simply because they were available. They were kept until most were either lost due to enemy action or became worn beyond repair. By then it was 1916 and the Allied light machine guns were being encountered on an increasing scale. The potential of the light machine gun had by then become more apparent to the German staff echelons so the leMG08/15 appeared (*see* Chapter 4). Surviving Madsen guns then underwent

another transfer of front to northern Italy where they were issued to Gebirgsjäger (mountain troops) battalions.

The Danish Madsen concern continued to sell its products to both the Allied and Central Powers during the World War I. During 1915 Austro-Hungary purchased 632 examples chambered for 6.5mm ammunition (later rechambered in Austria to 7.92mm). Some of these were issued as aircraft guns, a role in which the Madsen gun was not considered particularly successful, although observers' guns did appear between the wars. By 1939 the only European armed forces still

The Madsen M1924	
Model	Madsen M1924
Calibre	8mm (0.315in)
Length	1,143mm (45in)
Weight	9.07kg (20lb)
Muzzle velocity	715m/s (2,350ft/sec)
Rate of fire	450rds/min
Feed	40-round box

fielding the Madsen gun were Denmark and Norway, although many remained in South America.

Following post-1945 attempts to replace the ageing and increasingly uncommercial Madsen gun (one was the gas-operated 7.62mm Madsen-Saetter machine gun of the late 1950s which failed to attract much attention), DISA finally withdrew from the firearms business in 1970. The company continues to manufacture items such as machine-gun mountings and bipods.

HOTCHKISS AGAIN

The French were early protagonists of the light machine gun, although they referred to their first example as a machine rifle. It was the Fusil Mitrailleur Hotchkiss mle 1909, a smaller, short-barrelled version of the original gas-operated Hotchkiss mle 1897. It had a butt stock and the action was cocked using a bolt handle in a manner similar to that for a rifle. The usual Hotchkiss barrel-cooling rings were replaced by fins.

In the process of generally reducing weight down to about 11.7kg (25.8lb), the mle 1909 mechanism was revised slightly, the main internal change being the replacement of the original side-locking lug by a contrivance termed a fermature nut. The bolt engaged this nut on closing and turned it slightly for locking. Externally, the Hotchkiss metal strip feed was reversed, operating from right to left and with the rounds clipped to the underside. This latter feature was to prove one of the mle 1909's main sources of troubles, as feeding the easily damaged strips reliably required special training and handling to make it operate efficiently.

Life in the World War I trenches did not suit the mle 1909, so gradually it was withdrawn from front-line use to be issued to other users, such as the artillery or to fortifications. After 1918 the mle 1909 was withdrawn.

The French Army was not the only customer for the mle 1909, as it was adopted in 1909 by the US Army. Having become aware of how far behind the US forces were in the field of machine-gun deployment once the Maxim Gun had been type-classified, the US ordnance authorities began a search for a lighter machine gun to equip cavalry and infantry forces. The Hotchkiss mle 1909 seemed to foot the bill satisfactorily and it was adopted as the 0.30 Benét-Mercié machine rifle, named after Benét and Mercié of the French Hotchkiss concern. The total production run carried out at the Springfield Arsenal was 1,170.

The Hotchkiss mle 1909 light machine gun as delivered to Greece.

A Hotchkiss mle 1909 mounted, for some reason, on a tripod.

More were manufactured by Colt. Both bipod and tripod mountings were available.

To say the Benét-Mercié was a success in US service would be incorrect. It suffered the usual fate of its time, in that it was regarded as a general nuisance to be issued to the odds and sods of any unit. An end result of this attitude was the infamous incident in 1916 during campaigning against Mexican guerrillas, when poorly trained soldiers were unable to load their Benét-Mercié machine rifles in the dark. This type of problem was solved by better training, but even that could not save the Benét-Mercié when it reached France in 1918. The US soldiers rapidly came to the same conclusion as the French, in that the Benét-Mercié was completely unsuited to the rough conditions of the trenches. They were all shipped home to be used only for training purposes. After 1918 all remaining Benét-Mercié machine rifles were disposed of by sales or scrapping.

The British also became mle 1909 users. By 1916 their requirements for light machine guns were such that it was decided to purchase the manufacturing rights for the mle 1909. Production in the UK was carried out at the Royal Small Arms Factory at Enfield Lock, the guns being chambered for the British 0.303 cartridge. Usually known as the Hotchkiss Mark 1, the first guns retained the awkward strip feed. When the guns were selected to arm early British tanks the thirty-round metal strips were replaced by three-round strips hinged together to form belts – guns with this feature became the Mark 1*. Most British guns were provided with a bipod and butt stock, although an unlikely looking miniature tripod was an option.

Most British Hotchkiss gun production went either to arm tanks or to the cavalry. After 1918 many were stockpiled, only to be dragged out

The Hotchkiss mle 1909	
Model	Hotchkiss mle 1909
Calibre	6.5mm (0.256in)
Length	1,190mm (46.85in)
Weight	11.7kg (25.8lb)
Muzzle velocity	740m/s (2,428ft/sec)
Rate of fire	500rds/min
Feed	30-round strips

again in 1940 when German invasion seemed imminent. The Home Guard then became Hotchkiss owners. By then Hotchkiss guns were deemed as obsolescent, even for Home Defence, so once the invasion scare had died down they were passed on to provide a better-than-nothing form of air defence for merchant ships and fishing boats. Hotchkiss guns were not declared as officially obsolete until 1946, but by then few can have remained in service.

CHAUCHAT

Following its defeat during the Franco-Prussian War of 1870–71, the French Army determined on revenge and the return of the lost provinces of Alsace and Lorraine. The French Army's determination was so pronounced that it decided upon a new set of tactics devised to ensure that the sheer momentum of an attack would overcome any opposition. Infantry would advance towards the enemy at any opportunity, close artillery support being provided by the rapid-firing 75mm mle 1897 field gun. Rather than have the infantry attack with rifles and bayonets alone, it was decided that some source of portable automatic fire would be required.

The solution emerged as the machine rifle. As officers were then reluctant to defer fire decisions to the lower ranks on any scale, they devised a strict 'walking fire' drill whereby shoulder-slung machine rifles would only be fired at the enemy from the hip in a short burst every so many paces. The intention was to encourage the enemy to keep their heads down and allow waves of infantry to approach close enough for them to employ their bayonets enthusiastically and the attack would prevail.

Anyone who had read reports of the carnage of the Russo-Japanese War, where similar attacks had been commonplace, would have realized the futility of such optimism. For some reason the French Army chose not to dwell upon inconvenient conclusions and pressed ahead, not only with

the massed-attack doctrines but also with the machine rifle to go with them. For this the French Services Techniques de l'Artillerie (STA) established a commission of four, one of whom, Colonel Chauchat, gave his name to the eventual design that was adopted in 1913 but not placed in series production until 1915 (by which time its original function was redundant). The names of the other commission members were Suterre, Ribeyrolle and Gladiator, hence the alternative name of CSRG.

The Chauchat operated on the so-called long-recoil system devised by a Hungarian, Rudolf Frommer. His system has been little used subsequently for it involved many components moving to and fro, including the complete bolt and barrel. These locked together during a rearwards recoil stroke that was longer than the length of the cartridge. The barrel was then released forward while the bolt followed, slamming home a fresh round. The resultant juddering motion made accurate firing almost impossible, a procedure not assisted by a bipod with flimsy steel-rod legs.

Overall, the Chauchat was awkward to handle, while matters were not helped by the provision of a half-moon box magazine under the receiver. This held 8 × 50R Lebel rifle cartridges, which the commission was forced to adopt in the name of supply standardization. These rimmed cartridges had a pronounced tapered case, hence the half-moon shape. As the magazine held only twenty rounds, some member of the commission no doubt realized that these would soon be expended and incorporated an indication of how many were left by providing holes in the magazine sides. It no doubt seemed a good idea at the time, but once in action the holes simply admitted dirt and debris into the system to create troubles. The moving parts and interior surfaces were also prone to the same hazards.

The end result was, to say the least, unsatisfactory. Although there were times when examples could work well, it was rarely possible to fire at anywhere near the intended cyclic rate of 250rds/min before something went wrong.

Ammunition jams were frequent and difficult to clear rapidly. An aluminium heat sink over the air-cooled barrel was therefore rarely necessary.

To add to the overall woes of the Chauchat, the entire project appears to have been carried out with the intention of the final weapon costing as little as possible. Consequently the Chauchat was hastily constructed using cheap, low-grade materials with the accent on quantity, not quality. Some observers have noted that the Chauchat was the first of the mass-produced weapons using steel stampings and rivets from numerous suppliers to be assembled at a central plant. This was only partially true. Subcontractor manufacturing standards were so poor that hand finishing was often necessary and component interchangeability was almost non-existent.

If all this were not enough, the whiff of chicanery still hangs over the entire Chauchat saga, with lucrative subcontracts being issued to dubious concerns with few reasons to commend them, other than social or political connections.

For the French Army the Chauchat was available at a time when light machine guns were desperately needed, the intended 'walking fire'

function having been assigned to history. The weapon did have the saving grace that it could be produced and issued rapidly, the final French Army total being about 225,000. Thus, by the time the USA entered the war in 1917, there were more than sufficient to issue to American troops as they arrived in France. Eventually the US Government paid for 15,918 Chauchat mle 1915s.

US soldiers had little option but to accept them (although they soon longed for something better), mainly as an inter-Allies relations measure at a time when little else was available. US Ordnance authorities, still inexperienced and with little direct knowledge of the realities of trench life, then went one step too far.

As mentioned above, the Chauchat mle 1915 was chambered for the 8mm Lebel rifle cartridge. The US Army decided that, for ammunition supply reasons, it would be useful to have the gun accept the US 0.30-06 cartridge. French industry was more than happy to oblige, so contracts for 29,000 were placed. The result was a disaster, the 0.30 M1918.

The US 0.30-06 cartridge was much more powerful than the 8mm Lebel and inflicted extra

An 8mm Chauchat mle 1915 showing the oddly contoured magazine.

This picture of the 8mm Chauchat mle 1915 clearly displays its awkward lines and simple, although crude, construction.

stresses on an already unreliable operating system, to the extent that M1918 breakages were even more frequent than before and spent-case extraction jams multiplied. Another shortcoming was the revised box magazine, which could hold only sixteen rounds after alterations for the 0.30-06 cartridge, too few for tactical comfort when the gun did work. Usually it did not. As the gun had to be almost completely stripped to clear most stoppages, most soldiers cleared them by simply discarding their M1918s and taking up some other weapon. By the time binding M1918 contracts were finally fulfilled the US Army had paid for 19,241, all of them destined to be reduced to scrap as soon as post-war opportunity allowed.

The French Army also discarded its mle 1915 Chauchats soon after 1918, although a few went to colonial forces. By 1939 all it had left were about 21,000 forming an emergency reserve. During the 1920s, no doubt as the result of accomplished sales techniques, Chauchats were sold to Belgium and Greece, the name Gladiator being applied to them, probably in an attempt to disguise their provenance. Chauchats turned up during the

Spanish Civil War and even as late as the mid-1960s, in Vietnam.

Time did not improve the Chauchat. It is now looked upon as perhaps the worst machine gun ever issued on any scale.

The Chauchat mle 1915	
Model	Chauchat mle 1915
Calibre	8mm (0.315in)
Length	1,143mm (45in)
Weight	9.2kg (20lb)
Muzzle velocity	700m/s (2,300ft/sec)
Rate of fire	250–300rds/min
Feed	20-round box

DARNE

As a contrast, the Darne machine gun became an important gun in many ways. One was its low cost and simple construction, introduced for two reasons. The first was that machine guns were expected to be needed in huge numbers for the planned 1919 offensives (which never happened), so ease and speed of production were very necessary. The second was that the St Etienne factory owned by Regis et Pierre Darne et Compagnie was equipped with only the most basic, elderly machinery. As the Darne concern had been awarded the contract to manufacture Lewis Guns for the French Air Force, it discovered the limitations of its manufacturing capabilities and so decided to attempt something simpler.

The first Darne machine gun appeared in 1916 but, with other priorities more pressing, little happened at that time. It was late 1918 before the simplicity of the Darne design attracted the French Army enough for it to place a large-scale production contract, only for this to be rescinded a few months later, following the Armistice.

Fortunately for Regis Darne his gun had already proved itself efficient, despite using manufacturing methods similar to those for the Chauchat. If anything, the Darne looked even more rough and ready, with little attention paid to finish or finesse. Yet it was reliable, perhaps the cheapest machine gun made until that time, and had a high rate of fire (up to 1,700rds/min with the 7.5mm cartridge). It was the fire rate that attracted many air forces during the 1920s and 1930s, so the Darne was eventually employed more as an airborne gun than for land service.

The Darne was gas-operated, with an unusual ammunition feed system that has never been used since. Firing gas forces not only created the power to drive the gun, but also removed a fresh round from its linked belt as it travelled to the rear. The round was then cammed upwards to be chambered on the forward return of the bolt. The low-cost construction was such that there was not a single forged metal part in the entire gun (apart from the barrel), with all components formed from steel pressings.

French Army Darnes appear to have been mainly employed in North Africa.

By 1931 over 11,000 guns had been sold to Brazil, Czechoslovakia, Italy, Lithuania, Spain and Yugoslavia. Of these exports, the most significant were those to Spain, for production was carried out there by Unceta y Comania at Guernica. The Darne exactly met the demands of the Spanish Civil War and many were manufactured under primitive conditions and at an even lower cost than the French originals.

The Darne, little known now, heralded the manufacturing methods and processes that were to be employed on a much larger scale during the 1940s and after.

BAR

During the early years of the twentieth century, the US Army was much influenced by French Army doctrines and defence matters. Accordingly, US tacticians became exponents of adding massed-attack philosophies to their own tactics, although, thankfully, they never had the manpower or opportunity to carry them out. One detail of the French approach was the machine-rifle concept, which resulted in the Chauchat (*see above*), so that detail was also earmarked for adoption by the US Army as late as 1917, even though there were no funds and no suitable weapon to hand, or so it was thought.

Once again, John Browning was already well in advance of the market and had already devised a light and portable automatic weapon, the Browning Automatic Rifle, or BAR. The BAR appeared following Browning's own analysis of warfare on the Western Front, the path from sketches to hardware taking only a few months as he incorporated many features of his short-recoil mechanisms scaled down for the purpose.

By February 1917 Browning was ready to demonstrate his BAR, along with the machine gun that became the M1917. The well-recorded demonstration at Capitol Heights (*see* Chapter 8) also featured the first examples of the BAR. It attracted as much attention as the machine gun. Ordnance personnel placed verbal orders almost before the propellant fumes had died away. Type classification as the M1918 followed.

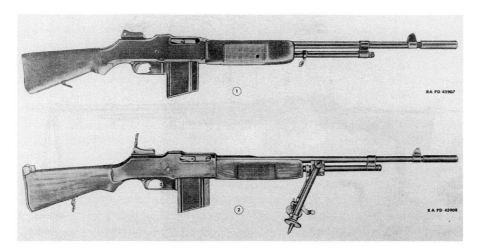

Two illustrations of the Browning Automatic Rifle (BAR), the top showing the original 0.30 M1918 and the lower the 0.30 M1918A1.

The M1918 BAR followed the machine-rifle concept to the letter. Weighing in at about 7.25kg (16lb) unloaded, it was designed to fire the standard 0.30-06 rifle cartridge on either single shot or automatic (at 550rds/min). Ammunition was fed from a twenty-round box. As the BAR was designed to be fired from the hip, supported by a shoulder sling, there was no bipod. Users soon learned that it was possible to fire from the shoulder but the recoil forces were not comfortable and bursts had to be short, especially as there was no barrel cooling or method of changing hot barrels.

BAR production was given a high priority but it took time to set up the necessary production facilities, even though John Browning had, as usual, designed his BAR with mass production in mind. Colt's was asked to prepare drawings plus the necessary special tools and gauges as well as establish a production line at its Hartford, Connecticut, premises. As Colt's was already very busy with other high-priority contracts further orders were placed with the Winchester Repeating Firearms Company and the Marlin-Rockwell Corporation, both at New Haven, also in Connecticut. The first production examples appeared during February 1918. By July 1918 the production total had reached 17,000, and by the time

World War I ended the total had swelled to 52,238 out of an intended 288,174.

It was late September 1918 before the first BARs saw action in France and they immediately became a great favourite, especially as the unloved Chauchats were all that had previously been available to the US infantry. Combat experience established the BAR as the 'centre of fire' of every combat squad, providing fire support for both attack and defence. The BAR proved reliable and easy to handle, the one apparent drawback being the limited magazine capacity of twenty rounds. BAR users therefore became adept at keeping bursts very short, using single shots wherever possible. Keeping the fire control switch on automatic became the norm for, with practice, the relatively slow rate of fire enabled single shots to be 'squeezed off'.

The ready acceptance of the BAR disguised the fact that it was really an odd hybrid weapon somewhere between the machine-rifle concept and the light machine gun. Exactly how it was categorized mattered little, for by the time of the Armistice the BAR was so well established that it remained in US service until the late 1950s.

During 1919 large numbers were returned to the Springfield Armory and placed into store, still unused and surplus to post-war requirements. By the 1930s a low-key enhancement programme was under way to produce the M1918A1, mainly involving the introduction of a bipod and a butt strap to provide firing stability when in the prone position.

During the 1920s and 1930s BARs were sold commercially to police and prison organizations. More were either exported or were the results of licence production, for the BAR made a considerable impression on many overseas observers. The BAR was manufactured in Belgium, Poland and Sweden, the Swedes introducing an interchangeable barrel system to their 6.5mm m/37, the successor to their original 6.5mm m/21.

The Poles adopted the BAR to fire 7.92 × 57mm ammunition and added a heavier finned barrel. Polish production of the wzor (model) 1928 was relatively slow, 10,715 having been issued to the Polish Army by 1939. Soon after, Polish BARs were absorbed into the German inventory and reissued to garrison units.

Browning's long association with Fabrique Nationale (FN) of Liège, Belgium, virtually guaranteed licence production there, so between the wars the FN plant churned out export models to China and Chile as well as for the Belgian armed forces. The Belgians also introduced a bipod and an interchangeable barrel system. As the FN plant emerged little damaged from the 1940–45 years, after 1945 the Belgian BAR was soon back in the marketplace. It remained so, with little success,

until 1967, although a few late production FN guns did end up in Egypt and with the newly formed Israeli armed forces.

To return to the Springfield Armory stockpile that virtually vanished during 1940. During the post-Dunkirk period, 25,000 of the original unmodified M1918 examples were shipped to the UK to arm what became the Home Guard – the BAR was never adopted by the regular UK armed forces, despite exhaustive testing of a 0.303in version during the 1920s and 1930s. That left the US stockpile virtually empty when the USA entered the war in December 1941, with the result that BAR production had to start all over again.

This time a new model was introduced. It was the M1918A2, complete with a bipod located further forward, a revised flash hider, a stock rest, and a new dual-rate fire-selection mechanism for 300–450 or 500–650rds/min. A carrying handle was added later. Not all of these innovations were popular, the dual fire control being widely considered unnecessary as it was difficult to clean and added something extra to go wrong. However, from 1941 onwards it was the M1918A2 or nothing.

M1918A2 production was passed to US industrial concerns, with military authorities supervising matters. Six concerns, none of them with any prior experience of weapons manufacture, became the New England Small Arms Corporation, with numerous subcontractors supplying

Last of the line, the Browning Automatic Rifle (BAR) 0.30 M1918A2.

*A Belgian FN
7.65mm mle 1930
guarding a
fortification.*

them. The new corporation took time to organize, and so it was not until early 1943 that mass production could really begin. After then, BARs were churned out by the thousand, the final late 1945 tally being 188,380.

Before the end of 1944 it was finally appreciated that popular though the BAR was with its users, better light fire support weapons were to hand. The immediate response was the unwieldy 0.30 M1919A6 (*see* Chapter 8). Many serving troops were also less than happy with the weight

and bulk of the M1918A2 BAR. Within many airborne and other special forces units the BAR lost its bipod, flash hider and other accessories to make it less of a load, but for most users the BAR was left unchanged.

The BAR remained in service throughout the Korean War. Before that war started, so many war-surplus BARs had been handed out to nations within the US sphere of influence that the BAR had to be put back into production yet again, this time by the Royal McBee Typewriter Company,

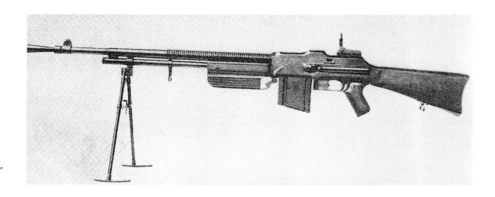

*The Polish 7.92mm
wzor 1928, a BAR
manufactured under
licence.*

which manufactured a further 61,000 or so. But even before that production run had been completed the writing was on the wall. The BAR was finally phased out of US service from 1957 onwards, the National Guard retaining its stock until a few years later. The French Army retained BARs for its campaigns in South-East Asia, some of which turned up in Vietcong hands as late as the 1970s.

The Bar M1918	
Model	BAR M1918
Calibre	0.30in (7.62mm)
Length	1,194mm (47in)
Weight	7.26kg (16lb)
Muzzle velocity	855m/s (2,805ft/sec)
Rate of fire	550rds/min
Feed	20-round box

12 The Lewis Gun

The gun that became perhaps the most successful of all the early light machine guns had its origins in unfortunate circumstances. The Lewis Gun was originally nothing to do with Colonel Isaac Newton Lewis, the man who gave the gun his name. Instead, it was the McClean Automatic Musket, or Musket Machine Gun, one of the many brainchildren of Doctor Samuel Neal McClean.

McClean was yet another American polymath, being a medical practitioner with a bent for inventing things, including automatic weapons. In 1900 he decided to devote himself to his inventions and formed the McClean Arms Company of New Jersey. The items produced were several, including heavy automatic weapons such as a one-pounder pom-pom carried on the back of a truck, but that failed to attract much attention. He then went on to a rifle-calibre Musket Machine Gun, a gas-operated, water-cooled weapon with ammunition fed from an overhead drum magazine.

The gun was also not a success. Problems arose from the gas cylinder that contained the piston driven to the rear by propellant gases tapped off from the barrel. During firing the cylinder became so hot that the associated return coil springs and some other components lost their strength and broke, causing jams. Subsequently, in yet another example of an inventor being unable to keep pace with the business side of things, McClean gradually lost control of his company. Before that happened, Lewis had appeared on the scene.

Lewis was a career soldier with an artillery background and yet another American with a positive attitude towards inventing things and making

them work. He had already filed a number of patents on devices ranging from rangefinders to electrical components. As a serving officer he could receive few financial gains from these patents, even though some did become commercial successes, but his attempts to promote his inventions and his abilities created difficulties within the strictly regulated US Army hierarchy. This was to cause Lewis problems in the future.

Lewis eventually came into contact with McClean after the collapse of McClean's first company. Executives from the resurrected McClean Arms & Ordnance Company approached Lewis with a view to him presenting a report on the viability of the McClean designs, and the Musket Machine Gun in particular. Lewis's report was favourable, this early association gradually blossoming to the point where Lewis became more and more involved with the gun's development, both on an engineering basis and in corporate terms.

By late 1909 it seemed that the McClean Company was destined for closure, but another approach to Lewis resulted in a decision to abandon the original water-cooling feature in favour of air-cooling. Lewis proposed an early outline of what he termed 'air ejection', whereby muzzle blast would draw cooling air from the chamber end and forwards through a barrel jacket. The jacket enclosed fins that absorbed barrel heat, exposing it to the cooling effects of the 'air ejection'. Further development was required before the spring heating problem was solved by introducing a clock return spring in a housing in front of the pistol grip.

Everyone's idea of what a Lewis Gun should look like, although the carrying handle on this example indicates that it is a 6.5mm variant delivered to Holland in 1920.

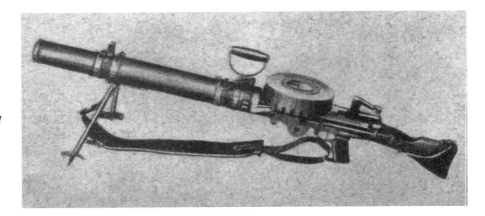

The three main features of the Lewis Gun were by then in place: the overhead drum; the air-cooling jacket; and the return spring housing. By late 1910 Lewis became actively involved with the newly named Automatic Arms Company (AAC) by signing a two-year contract and taking extended leave to carry out further gun development.

PROSPECTS

As the manufacturing facilities of the AAC were limited to small workshops it was decided to pass the basic design, already renamed the Lewis Gun, to the Savage Arms Company of New York. That concern already had close contacts with the US Government regarding small arms manufacturing, so it was hoped that the Lewis Gun manufactured by them would find favour with what was then seen as the most likely customer, the US Government.

It was not to be. All manner of obstacles were placed in the way of the US Army testing the gun, many apparently instigated by Brigadier General Crozier, Chief of the Bureau of Ordnance. It appears that Crozier had not forgotten the resentments caused by the forceful Major Lewis when previously promoting his inventive abilities. The Crozier/Lewis relationship soon became acrimonious, Crozier doing his best to block any testing, or even tenuous consideration, of the Lewis Gun by the US Army.

The future course of this dispute became apparent when one of the first Lewis Guns manufactured by Savage was fired from an airborne Wright Pusher biplane against a ground target, the first known firing of a machine gun while in flight. The demonstration created quite a stir in the press, but the Ordnance Board refused to countenance any notion of arming US Army aircraft.

The blocking of the local military market might have discouraged many individuals but Lewis simply took his gun elsewhere. As with so many American machine-gun pioneers, Lewis turned to Europe. Almost at once, two associations transformed the Lewis Gun's prospects. One was with the British Birmingham Small Arms Company (BSA), and the other with Belgian military authorities.

Taking the BSA situation first, the British company was looking for some way to break into the automatic weapon market. They sponsored a Lewis Gun demonstration for British staff officers, including aircraft firings, but as the British had already opted for the Vickers Gun there seemed to be few further openings there. Further demonstrations in Belgium led to so much interest from the Belgian authorities that they requested a manufacturing facility be established within

Belgium to meet local demand. Despite the formation of a European ACC holding company (Armes Automatique Lewis), attempts to establish such a facility within Belgium eventually came to nothing, for a variety of reasons, commercial, political and otherwise, but the BSA avenue remained open.

During 1913 Lewis established a licence production agreement with BSA. Under Colonel Lewis's personal supervision, BSA took over the remaining pre-production development still needed prior to meeting the first Belgian order for fifty guns. That same year also witnessed yet more demonstrations to numerous British authorities, resulting in the lukewarm approval of a 0.303in model with a forty-seven-round drum magazine. However, it was considered that the Lewis Gun would prove more useful for aircraft installations rather than land service.

ACCEPTANCE

Initial Lewis Gun production by BSA was limited to meeting export orders. That situation had been transformed by the end of 1914. The start of World War I found the British armed forces short of virtually everything, with machine guns high on the priority list. As BSA was already in a position to supply Lewis Guns, the type was therefore officially adopted and ordered in quantity, more as an expedient than as a long-term measure. There was no policy to utilize the Lewis Gun as a light machine gun, for that concept had scarcely been considered, although the Lewis became a general infantry issue rather than a specialized weapon, as with the Vickers Gun. In truth, the Lewis was not particularly light at about 12.25kg (27lb).

By mid-1915 BSA was producing 150 guns each week, although that was soon to prove insufficient. Not only were the British armed forces expanding at an unprecedented rate, and had to be equipped, but the Lewis Gun proved to be highly popular with those who received the type, both for air and ground use.

Front-line troops found the Lewis Gun to be highly adaptable. The portability of the gun during the rough and tumble of trench warfare made it much more user-friendly and accessible than the heavier, resource-demanding Vickers Gun, despite the latter's abilities to produce massive amounts of fire. Once the limited burst capabilities of the Lewis became accepted (a cyclic 375 to 600 rds/min depending on the setting of a variable-position gas port), demands for more and yet more began to arrive from all fronts.

BSA manufacturing facilities had to be greatly expanded as World War I progressed, yet demands still could not be met. Not only were Lewis Guns needed to equip new formations and aircraft squadrons, but front-line losses proved far more than anticipated. In addition, as more and more guns reached the front lines, the hard life of the trenches led to a corresponding need for spare parts in huge quantities, especially for the drum magazines that were to prove the Lewis Gun's major shortcoming. Drum distortions and related damage inevitably led to stoppages, while components such as return springs frequently needed replacement. By the end of 1915 arrangements had been made for Lewis Guns to be manufactured in the USA, by the (by then reorganized) Savage Arms Corporation that had made the first Lewis Guns in 1910. By the end of 1915 an initial order for 10,000 had been placed. More Savage-produced guns were to follow.

LARGE SCALE

By the end of 1917 the Lewis Gun had become so accepted by British Army infantry units that many infantry platoons had somehow acquired their own integral Lewis Gun fire support. In addition to its usual duties, Lewis Guns were also adapted to be anti-aircraft guns, while the number of aircraft gun installations became so many that production for airborne installations came to rival that for ground use.

For aircraft installations the bulky cooling arrangements were not necessary, so guns were manufactured without them. Another important development for airborne installations, apart from spade grips, was the introduction of a ninety-seven-round drum in place of the usual forty-seven-round item. Much of the American 'Savage Lewis' production output was for aircraft. By the time Savage production for the UK was wound down in December 1918, 39,200 aircraft guns had been completed, compared to 2,500 guns for land service. Another 1,050 guns were chambered for British 0.303 ammunition and retained for training in the USA.

By the time the war ended BSA was producing 1,500 Lewis Guns a week. BSA production totals by then had reached 145,397, many as replacements for combat losses. To these could be added the 52,000 or so made in the USA by Savage, although the major proportion of those was destined for Canada and the US Government.

NEW USERS

The Lewis Gun gradually spread to Commonwealth forces and even the French adopted the type for their aircraft. Lewis Guns for aircraft installations were manufactured in France by Regis et Pierre Darne et Compagnie at St Etienne. A total of 4,336 were made, all chambered for the British 0.303 cartridge, as the French 8mm Lebel cartridge proved unsuitable for the Lewis. More French guns came direct from the UK and the USA.

Further Lewis Guns went to Italy, Russia and Portugal. Even the Germans employed the Lewis, although their guns were captured examples. German Army units were so anxious to adopt the Lewis that instruction manuals were prepared and issued, while front-line stretcher bearers were ordered to collect any examples found and carry them to the rear along with the casualties.

Sales to the US Government had a somewhat troubled history. Even after it was appreciated that the US machine-gun supply situation was desperate, Ordnance Board officials continued to hold out against adopting the Lewis Gun – the old Crozier/Lewis antipathies had apparently not been forgotten. That logjam was finally broken when the US Marine Corps adopted the Lewis in April 1917, the guns being chambered for the US 0.30-06 cartridge.

It was not until late 1917, when the US Army realized it was to become involved in the fighting in France, that substantial American orders (for an initial 42,000 guns, later increased to 86,700) were placed with Savage for the US Army. By that time, production by Savage was already progressing at such a pace that resources to meet these extra orders were difficult to establish. Even so, over 16,000 0.30 Savage Lewis Guns were delivered to the US Government by May 1918.

Few US Lewis Guns made it to France. Any that did arrive were subsequently withdrawn and replaced with Hotchkiss or Chauchat guns to keep logistics tidy.

The totals mentioned above indicate that the Lewis Gun was numerically one of the most important of all contemporary machine guns, second numerically only to the unloved Chauchat. Unfortunately, the Lewis Gun was destined to play major roles in other wars.

INTERWAR ADOPTIONS

As with so much other war materiel, Lewis Gun production, both in the UK and USA, had tapered away to nothing by the end of 1918, leaving enough guns to meet all likely requirements for years to come. Some interwar export production did take place, but for BSA the post-war emphasis was on general development and product improvement, including a 0.50 variant. All the development activity was rendered of little value due to the adoption of the Bren Gun (*see* Chapter 14) by the British Army during the late 1930s. In the same manner, efforts to increase the cyclic fire

Back in business, a twin-gun Lewis Gun mounting for air defence in 1940.

rate for flexible-mounting aircraft guns were largely negated by the adoption of the Vickers GO gun (*see* Chapter 13).

During the interwar years the Lewis Gun was adopted by several nations other than the pre-1918 users. While not strictly speaking post-war, mention must be made of the Lewis Gun in Russia. Prior to 1917 about 1,000 were ordered, chambered for the local 7.62 × 54R cartridge, to be retained throughout the Russian Civil War, some ending up in Polish hands. They were never regarded as a success as they were considered too flimsy to meet local conditions, although design features taken from the Lewis were subsequently incorporated into several post-1920 Soviet machine-gun ventures.

By the end of 1918 the Dutch had decided to adopt the Lewis Gun, mainly as the result of testing guns taken from Lewis-armed British or French aircraft that had strayed into neutral Holland. Following a few minor modifications, production of the subsequent M.20 (from the year of introduction, 1920) took place in Holland at the State Arsenal Artillerie Inrichtingen in Zaandam. Numerous M.20 sub-variants appeared for the Dutch armed forces and for colonial duties in what is now Indonesia. Dutch Lewis Guns were placed on ground bipods and tripods, motor cycles, aircraft (without the cooling sleeve), armoured cars and light naval craft. Most M.20s fired the standard Dutch 6.5 × 53.5R rifle cartridge, although from 1925 onwards guns were

Interwar experiment, a Lewis four-gun mounting with air-cooled barrels – the carrier vehicle is a Morris-Commercial D 6 × 4 30cwt truck.

modified to accommodate the 7.92 × 57R cartridge of German origin.

M.20 production appears to have assumed a languid pace, for by early 1940 the Dutch armed forces had stocks of about 8,500, still some way short of their planned requirements. After the Germans invaded in May 1940 the Dutch production line was captured virtually intact so production for the conquerors was maintained until the end of the year. Dutch trophy guns, captured and newly manufactured, were not adopted by the German armed forces as a front-line weapon. Instead, they were handed out to second-line and occupation garrison units as the 6.5mm MG 100(h). (Captured British examples were the

7.7mm MG137(e).) A few were still around in 1945, the last being issued to Volksturm home defence units.

The Japanese also adopted the Lewis Gun. They had been interested in the gun ever since 1913, but it was not until 1929 that the first batch was delivered from the UK to the Japanese Navy. Local production rights were negotiated and assumed by Japanese Government arsenals at Toyokawa, Yokosuka and Hiratsuka. The first such guns were completed during 1932, hence the Japanese Type 92 designation according to the local calendar. Most Type 92s were chambered for a 7.7mm cartridge based on the British 0.303. Production continued in several land, naval and

One of the 0.30 Savage Lewis aircraft guns delivered to the UK in 1940 and later converted for ground use.

aircraft forms until 1945, making the Japanese guns the last Lewis Guns in production.

Other Lewis Gun users after 1918 included Czechoslovakia, Poland and Finland.

ANOTHER WAR

By the time the World War II commenced the British Army had adopted the Bren Gun, so any Lewis Guns still around had been placed in

reserve, other than some aircraft guns. Things altered drastically after the Dunkirk evacuation of May–June 1940, for the major portion of the British Army's weapon inventory was left behind in France, including virtually all the front-line machine-gun holdings. Although machine-gun production facilities were by then working over-time, Home Defence and many other formations had to be rapidly provided with new weapons. It was time for the remaining Lewis Guns to be taken back into service.

Two 0.30 Savage Lewis guns still being deployed as low-level air defence weapons during 1942.

The surviving 2,500 or so Bren Guns were retained for front-line divisions, leaving the old 0.303 Lewis Guns for Home Defence and the defence of RAF airfields and related installations. To boost numbers to hand, recourse was made to the USA and its warehoused 0.30 Savage Lewis Guns. In time, 38,040 of these guns were shipped across the Atlantic, originally by purchase but eventually by Lease-Lend. Most of the 0.30 weapons were destined for the Home Guard.

As most of the 0.30 Savage Lewis Guns supplied had been manufactured for aircraft installations, they were initially unsuitable for land use. When first delivered, the desperately needed Savage Lewis Guns were issued as they were, without bipods or any other mounting. Local improvisations to offset this shortcoming were hastily introduced, including rudimentary skeleton butts and bipods. One aircraft gun situation that could not be addressed was that Savage Lewis barrels lacked the cooling sleeve. This never appears to have led to any major problems, giving rise to thoughts of whether the usual Lewis cooling system was necessary at all.

Apart from the Home Guard, numbers of Lewis and Savage Lewis Guns passed to what were normally end-of-the line users, such as merchant ships and fishing boats requiring some form of air defence. In 1940 and early 1941, many such vessels received just one Lewis Gun to defend themselves, although matters gradually improved as the war continued.

The Lewis Gun had been used for air defence prior to 1918, but the events of 1940 and after demonstrated that it was in many ways a better anti-aircraft weapon than the Bren. The Bren box magazine could hold only twenty-nine rounds, which were soon expended during any engagement. The Lewis Gun had a forty-seven- or even a ninety-seven-round drum magazine. This extra capacity proved far more useful when engaging aircraft targets, especially when twin or quadruple air defence mountings could be issued. One record from the Battle of Britain period states that one low-flying German aircraft in five brought down over the UK was a Lewis Gun victim.

The Lewis Gun was finally declared obsolete in British service during 1946, although few remained by then.

A captured Japanese, tripod-mounted 7.7mm Type 97.

Even though this rather poor quality 1940 illustration is somewhat blurred, the distinctive shape of the Lewis Gun stands out. The picture denotes Dutch troops defending their national borders in 1940.

HEFAH

One of the least known of all Lewis Gun derivatives is the 0.303 Hefah – few references even mention it. It was an exercise in making the Lewis Gun as rapidly and simply as possible and was originally a 1940 private venture by the Ductile Steel Company of Short Heath, Staffordshire. They simplified the basic Lewis mechanism and placed the magazine under the much-modified receiver. The result was officially deemed barely satisfactory, but such was the need for any sort of machine gun in 1940 that it was ordered into production. Unfortunately, there was no manufacturing facility with capacity to spare so it was not until 1942 that the Hefah Company of Wednesfield, Staffordshire, could deliver the first examples.

The main recipients were the Royal Navy, which mounted them in pairs on light coastal craft. The Merchant Navy also received the Hefah. Exactly how many Hefahs were made has yet to be uncovered, but it cannot have been many. The type was officially declared obsolete in November 1944.

FINALE

During 1948 yet another Lewis Gun operator appeared, this time the newly emergent state of Israel. Lewis Guns had been issued to British-controlled Jewish police and military units for years before then, but by 1948 unknown numbers had somehow passed into Israeli hands. More came from various unrecorded sources. The numbers were never large. They were employed during the early national survival campaigns against local Arab nations but were replaced as soon as could be managed. They were the last Lewis Guns known to have seen active service.

The Lewis Gun	
Model	Lewis Gun (British)
Calibre	0.303in (7.7mm)
Length	1,250mm (49.2in)
Weight	12.15kg (27lb)
Muzzle velocity	744m/s (2,440ft/sec)
Rate of fire	450rds/min
Feed	47- or 97-round drum

13 Between the Wars

After 1918 it seemed the world was sated with machine guns. The soldiers went home, defence budgets dwindled and production lines closed down. Armouries were stacked full of machine guns that, it was then anticipated, would never be used on any scale again. For a few years machine-gun developments were almost non-existent.

Yet here and there things were happening. Within several nations a few dedicated officers were doing their best to analyse the lessons of the World War I, preparing for the conflict that, even during the 1920s, many forecast was still to come. The German Army was in the vanguard of this movement to the extent that its contributions are outlined in a separate chapter (Chapter 16). Several other nations did manage to carry out some machine-gun work, one of them being France.

FRANCE

The French Army had been very impressed by the Browning Automatic Rifle (*see* Chapter 11), at one time considering large-scale purchases to replace the unloved mle 1915 Chauchat (*also see* Chapter 11). That intention could not be fulfilled until the US Army had received its backlog of BAR orders from hard-pressed manufacturers, so the French never received anything other than a small trials batch before the war ended and the need for new guns was no longer pressing. But something better than the Chauchat was still needed.

Examination of those few BARs drove home the lesson that the old 8mm Lebel cartridge was unsuitable for future machine-gun applications.

A new cartridge was therefore devised. This emerged as the 7.5 × 58mm mle 1924, with an immediate application in the Fusil Mitrailleur mle 1924 developed at the Manufacture Nationale d'Armes de Châtellerault. The mle 1924, the prototype for which was ready during 1921 despite funding difficulties, was basically a BAR but with a few Gallic touches such as two triggers, the front for single shots, the other for automatic. The twenty-five-round box magazine was moved to the top and there were some other detail changes, including provision to secure a monopod support under the butt stock, although this was rarely used.

The mle 1924 was tested in combat in North Africa almost as soon as it was first issued. Problems arose immediately regarding the ammunition. It seems the propellant charge was too powerful for the gun, something compounded by the cartridge's close visual similarity to German 7.92 × 57mm Mauser ammunition taken over by the French after 1918 and consumed during low-cost training with captured German weapons. It seems that 7.5 and 7.92mm cartridges got mixed together. Whatever the reason, mle 1924 guns experienced a series of exploding barrels that did little to impart user confidence.

The eventual solution was a less powerful cartridge, the shorter 7.5 × 54mm mle 1929C. The Châtellerault mle 1924 had to be modified accordingly, resulting in the mle 1924/29, which then settled down to become the accepted French light machine gun and one of the best available when 1939 came around. By then, nearly 60,000 had been manufactured or were on order.

A 7.5mm Châtellerault mle 1924/29, clearly displaying its Browning Automatic Rifle origins.

By 1939 a variant had appeared, the mle 1931, originally intended for the Maginot Line fortifications. The mle 1931 featured a prominent, side-mounted (left or right) 150-round drum magazine, a heavy barrel, provision for installation in armoured mantlets, and an oddly contoured butt. Another odd characteristic on the fortification mle 1931 was the addition of a cooling system that sprayed a water jet into the chamber between rounds, the intention being that long bursts could then be fired without the barrel overheating. A thirty-six-round box magazine formed an alternative to the bulky drum.

In time, the mle 1931 spread to armoured vehicle installations and air defence mountings where the extra drum capacity was considered a great advantage over contemporary designs. There was also a mle 1934 aircraft gun for fixed or

A side view of a magazineless 7.5mm Châtellerault mle 1924/29.

An indication of the cost, complexity and ruggedness of this twin-gun 7.5mm Châtellerault mle 1931 installation can be seen from this dismounted Maginot Line example.

flexible mountings and a mle 1939 with a belt feed. Châtellerault mle 1924/29 guns also ended up in the Maginot Line defences.

Châtellerault mle 1924/29	
Model	Châtellerault mle 1924/29
Calibre	7.5mm (0.295in)
Length	1,007mm (39.65in)
Weight	8.93kg (19.69lb)
Muzzle velocity	820m/s (2,690ft/sec)
Rate of fire	450–600rds/min
Feed	25-round box

After mid-1940 the mle 1924/29 and mle 1931 entered the German inventory, employed mainly by occupation units in France. After 1945, events in French Indo-China meant that the mle 1924/29 was placed back into production at Châtellerault, the line finally closing during 1950. Many of these late-production mle 1924/29s (and tripod- or pintle-mounted mle 1931s) ended up in Vietcong hands.

VICKERS-BERTHIER

Although the Vickers-Berthier light machine gun could trace its design origins back to 1908, it was not until the 1930s that it achieved any degree

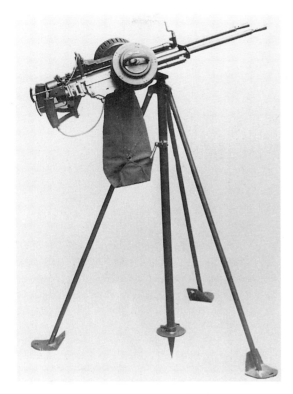

Although originally intended as a fortification and tank weapon, the 7.5mm Châtellerault mle 1931 was frequently deployed in the low-level air defence role, as this twin-gun mounting indicates.

of prominence. In 1908 one Lieutenant André Berthier produced a light machine gun to meet what he perceived as an urgent requirement for infantry squads to have their own fire support. His first model was unusual in many ways, for despite being gas-operated it had a water-cooled barrel. A tight-fitting jacket around the barrel was constantly refilled with water by a small, circulating hand pump operated by an assistant. This system permitted a cyclic fire rate of 600rds/min and was backed up by a system that enabled barrel changing within seconds. The gas operation was along the same lines as many other similar designs (especially the Browning Automatic Rifle), with gas tapped from the barrel to drive the

gun mechanisms. Ammunition was fed from an overhead box magazine. The gun worked reliably with a noticeably smooth operation.

Arrangements were made to manufacture the Berthier gun at the Pieper factory at Herstal in Belgium, without immediate commercial success. The French Army did not adopt the type, selecting instead the dreadful Chauchat, no doubt for production reasons. Thanks to a lack of funding and facilities, the Berthier gun was hardly suitable for mass production when it was needed most and so, despite attempts to interest the US military in the design, it seemed the Berthier design was destined to fade away.

In 1925 the situation changed. Vickers of the UK was then running out of work at its Crayford factory and was looking for a foothold in the light machine-gun market. The company therefore acquired the manufacturing rights to the Berthier, thereafter known as the Vickers-Berthier. By then, the gun had an air-cooled barrel and a thirty-round overhead box magazine. Although the market was overcrowded at that time, Vickers was soon making commercial sales to countries such as Spain, while several South American nations acquired batches. The largest sales were to the Indian Army, a semi-autonomous organization with its own procurement infrastructure. That was in 1933, with the first batches being supplied by Vickers before local production started in India at the Rifle Factory, Ishapore. The Indian Army therefore took the 0.303 Vickers-Berthier to war in 1939 and retained it until at least the mid-1970s, although by then it was a reserve weapon.

A late-production Vickers-Berthier Mark IIIB for the Indian Army.

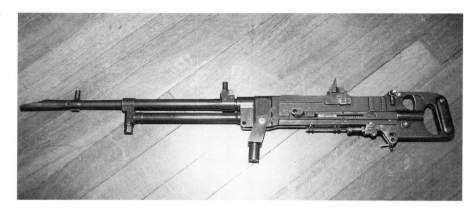

The aircraft-mounted Vickers GO gun.

At one point during the mid-1930s it seemed that the British Army would adopt the Vickers-Berthier to replace its Lewis Guns, but this was not to be. The Bren Gun was adopted instead (*see* Chapter 14). In fact, the Bren Gun gradually supplemented and then largely replaced the Vickers-Berthier within the Indian Army for, as enough came to hand, it allowed a higher degree of logistic standardization between armies, especially when operating in theatres such as Burma. Front-line formations were increasingly equipped with the Bren, while the Vickers-Berthier was passed to support and second-line units.

There was also an aircraft version of the Vickers-Berthier. Starting in 1928 Vickers undertook a virtual redesign of the basic Berthier gun to make it suitable for the aircraft observer's role. The result was the Vickers GO (Gas Operated) or Vickers K gun with spade grips, a top-mounted ninety-six-round (originally sixty-round) drum magazine, and easy access to items such as ejectors that might have to be changed while the host aircraft was in flight. The RAF did eventually adopt the type in 1939, but its service life was short. It arrived at a time when new aircraft were adopting power-driven gun turrets and the Vickers GO was not suitable for use within the close confines of a turret. In 1943 the Vickers GO was officially declared obsolete, although the Fleet Air Arm continued to use them on aircraft such as the Swordfish until the war ended.

As the Vickers GO guns were withdrawn they were passed to the Royal Navy, where they were adapted for low-level air defence. The Army also received the type and with them it acquired a novel role. In North Africa they were adopted by the various 'private armies' that proliferated there to operate behind enemy lines. Liberally festooned around various types of cross-country vehicle, the Vickers GO proved highly successful as a general-purpose weapon.

DEGTYAREV

During World War I the Tsarist Army came to recognize the combat value of the light machine gun and attempted to field as many as it could obtain. Starting as early as 1905 with the Madsen, which at that time the Army regarded as simply another machine gun, the pre-1917 Army saddled itself

Vickers-Berthier Mark 3	
Model	Vickers-Berthier Mark 3
Calibre	0.303in (7.7mm)
Length	1,156mm (45.5in)
Weight	10.9kg (24.4lb)
Muzzle velocity	745m/s (2,450ft/sec)
Rate of fire	450–600rds/min
Feed	30-round box

with just about every type of portable machine gun it could purchase. This included Lewis Guns, Hotchkiss mle 1909s and even the mle 1915 Chauchat. These duly passed to the Red Army after 1917 to be used throughout the Civil War that followed. By the time that conflict was over, the Red Army was determined to have its own light machine gun, and have it in quantity.

None of the 'foreign' guns was considered suitable for the Red Army, being regarded as too flimsy, unreliable and complicated to serve under Soviet conditions. Attempts were made to rectify matters, including making lightened Maxim Guns (*see* Chapter 5), but they were unsuccessful. Consideration was then given to a novel design from one Vasiliy Degtyarev, a talented gunsmith at the Tula Arsenal.

As early as 1924, Degtyarev had proposed a gas-operated light machine gun. It soon attracted attention due to its light weight of just over 9kg (20lb), simplicity and a minimum of components (just sixty-five) to be manufactured. The Degtyarev gun underwent a prolonged series of rigorous trials that involved sending the guns back to the workshops several times for modifications to make them more rugged, amenable to operation under extreme environmental conditions and easier to maintain. The trials and modification period lasted until 1928 before the gun was ordered as the 7.62mm Pulemet Degtyareva Pekhotnii, or DP. It turned out to be a durable and reliable winner.

The DP was simple to an extreme, enabling it to be manufactured with a minimum of machined components but using the best steel available. Ammunition was fed from an overhead flat pan

The original 7.62mm DP light machine gun.

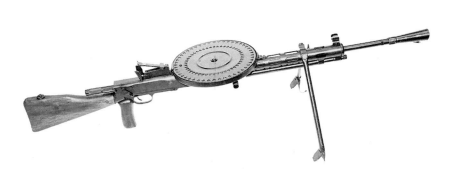

A direct comparison displaying the changes made to produce the 7.62mm DPM, the most obvious being the pistol grip and the spring tube extension protruding from the back of the receiver.

A Soviet Army 7.62mm DP light machine gun team in action.

magazine, originally intended for forty-nine rounds but later reduced to forty-seven to reduce the chances of misfeeds from the rimmed 7.62 × 54R ammunition. The drum did prove to be rather prone to damage and was one of the DP's less successful points, although it could continue to work under surprisingly harsh conditions. Fire was automatic only, at a cyclic rate of 500–600 rds/min, the Red Army seeing no logic in a machine gun firing single shots, thereby simplifying the design and reducing the number of items that might go wrong.

Production of the DP began at Tula in 1930 and it was churned out in thousands. A tank version, the DT, was developed with a heavier barrel, sixty-round magazine and a rudimentary butt and bipod for dismounted use. There were also two aircraft models, the DA and twin DA-2. The DP was first used in action during the Spanish Civil War, on the Republican side.

The DP did have its shortcomings but they were few, although one was eventually to lead to a redesign. In common with many other gas-operated designs, the gas piston and return spring were located under the barrel. As the barrel was air-cooled and could not be changed easily, it could

get very hot, especially when cooling fins were omitted after 1941 to speed production. During prolonged firing the return spring often became heated to the point where it lost its strength and caused malfunctions. Ventilation holes were introduced along the spring housing, but this was only a partial solution. Only a redesign could overcome the fault and so it had to be endured during a period when mass production to counter the German invasion was more urgent than technical perfection.

The redesign appeared in 1944, relocating the return spring to a position behind the bolt, necessitating an elongated housing over the small of the butt where the firer normally gripped the gun.

DP	
Model	DP
Calibre	7.62mm (0.30in)
Length	1,265mm (49.8in)
Weight	11.9kg (26.23lb)
Muzzle velocity	844m/s (2,770ft/sec)
Rate of fire	520–580rds/min
Feed	47-round drum

Another view of the 7.62mm DPM.

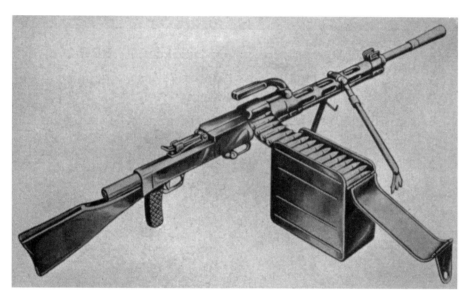

The post-war 7.62mm RP-46, a DPM converted to belt feed.

A pistol grip therefore had to be added. At the same time, the bipod became a fixture and was strengthened as well. The result was the Pulemet Degtyareva Pekhotnii Modificatsionii 1944, thankfully usually abbreviated to just DPM. The same modifications were introduced for the tank-borne DTM. (By 1944 there was no longer any useful role for the airborne DA to perform.)

After 1945 the DP, DPM, DT and DTM served on for many years with the Warsaw Pact armies, plus many others under Soviet influence. The DPM may still be encountered today in odd corners around the world. The Communist Chinese copied the DPM as their Type 53.

There was one final addition to the Degtyarev family and that entered service in 1946. A belt feed mechanism was introduced, retaining the ability to use the DP/DPM pan magazine when required. The result was the 7.62mm RP-46 but the Red Army apparently made little use of it. The Communist Chinese did manufacture the RP-46 as their Type 58 and it was copied by the North Koreans (Type 64).

The Japanese 6.5mm Light Machine Gun Type 11, clearly showing the unusual ammunition hopper.

JAPAN

During the Russo-Japanese War of 1905–06 the Japanese Army became very interested in captured examples of the Danish Madsen and resolved to develop its own equivalent. Yet it was 1922 before an indigenous equivalent appeared in the odd shape of the odd 6.5mm Type 11, or Juichi nenskiki keikikanju. The Type 11 was designed and developed by the Nambu Armament Manufacturing Company of Tokyo and was based around Hotchkiss operating principles, although it had some features all of its own.

Perhaps the oddest of these was the ammunition feed, based on a thirty-round hopper on the left-hand side of the gun into which standard Arisaka rifle five-round ammunition clips could be stacked. Before rounds were fed into the gun they were stripped from their clips and oiled to assist spent-case extraction. The idea certainly simplified ammunition supply, but the mechanism was complicated and induced constant troubles, further compounded by the oiling feature that attracted dust and dirt. Even so, the Soviets were sufficiently impressed with the idea to carry out trials with a suitably modified DP. Nothing came of that project.

Experience showed that the 6.5 × 51mm Arisaka cartridge was really too powerful for

An unusual top view of the Japanese 6.5mm Light Machine Gun Type 11, showing the ammunition hopper and the offset butt stock.

the extractor mechanism to handle, even with oiled cartridges. The only solution was to develop a special reduced-propellant charge specifically for use with the Type 11, doing away with the supply advantages that the hopper feed had been meant to provide and adding yet another cartridge type for Japanese quartermasters to worry about.

To add to the shortcomings of the Type 11, it was an awkward weapon to handle, something not helped by the distinctive and offset butt shape, and was no doubt rather expensive to manufacture and maintain. But Japanese soldiers learned to live with such matters and retained the Type 11 until 1945, after which the gun could be encountered throughout the Far East for several years.

The main Type 11 variant was the Type 91 tank machine gun with an enlarged fifty-round hopper and no butt stock. An optical sight was provided. Later in the war the Type 91 was often deployed on a bipod for infantry use.

After 1936 the Type 11 was joined in service by the 6.5mm Type 96. The Type 96 was meant to be the replacement for the Type 11, but this was never possible due to the limited capacity of the Japanese industrial base. The Type 96 mechanism managed to combine features from both the earlier Hotchkiss models and the Czech ZB26, but the oiling mechanism and the reduced power cartridge were carried over, although the Type 96 oiler was inside the receiver and thus less prone to the introduction of debris. A quick-change barrel was introduced, as was an optical sight and an overhead thirty-round box magazine.

The Type 96 may have been an improvement over the Type 11, but only slightly. The main shortcomings of both were done away with by the introduction of the 7.7mm Type 99. Not only was the 7.7×57mm cartridge more suitable for the machine-gun role, but it did not require oiling to ensure efficient extraction. Externally and internally there were few visual differences between

The 6.5mm Light Machine Gun Type 96 together with its optional shield, a most unusual light machine gun accessory – the 7.7mm Type 99 was visually very similar.

the 6.5mm Type 96 and the 7.7mm Type 99. Both could have bayonets installed, a most unusual capability for any machine gun. Another unusual accessory was an optional armoured shield.

Many observers considered the Type 99 to be the best of all the Japanese machine guns, light or heavy, although due to production delays relatively few reached the troops. After 1945 the type was retained by Chinese forces and, after reboring for 7.92 × 57mm ammunition, was retained in service for many years, seeing active service in Korea and Vietnam.

ITALY

As early as 1924 the Italian Army sponsored the development of a light machine gun from Breda. After a series of unsatisfactory models the 6.5mm modello 30 was finally adopted, although exactly why is difficult to determine. The product was a horror for numerous reasons.

For a start it appeared to have been put together by a committee. It had all manner of angular bits and pieces along its outline, all ready to snag on anything and create discomfort when firing or being carried – there was no provision for a sling or carrying handle. The perennial malfunction-inducing practice of oiling cartridges was retained, as the locking mechanism was a slightly modified but harsh form of blowback involving a relatively heavy bolt that needed a film of oil in the chamber to assist extraction. The ammunition feed was further complicated by the provision of a hinged magazine ready to be loaded from a cardboard or brass charger holding twenty rounds. As the magazine was a fixture on the gun, if it

Type 11	
Model	Type 11
Calibre	6.5mm (0.256in)
Length	1,105mm (43.5in)
Weight	10.1kg (22.5lb)
Muzzle velocity	700m/s (2,300ft/sec)
Rate of fire	500rds/min
Feed	30-round hopper

The angular lines of the Italian 6.5mm modello 30 light machine gun showing the side-mounted magazine arrangement.

Breda Modello 30

Model	Breda modello 30
Calibre	6.5mm (0.256in)
Length	1,232mm (48.5in)
Weight	10.24kg (22.75lb)
Muzzle velocity	629m/s (2,063ft/sec)
Rate of fire	450–500rds/min
Feed	20-round fixed box

was damaged or became distorted the entire gun became useless. To round off a bad design, changing a hot barrel was a complicated task made even more awkward by there being no provision to handle the hot barrel. As the modello 30 was among the first light machine guns to feature a quick-change barrel, such operational details were not appreciated by the designers.

In addition to all the above, the 6.5 × 52mm cartridge was under-powered, even for the light machine-gun role. Yet this combination was placed into series production to become the standard Italian light machine gun throughout the Second World War. There was an attempt to update the design by rechambering for a 7.35 × 51mm cartridge, but few were manufactured. However, for all its faults the modello 30 was all the Italian Army had, and so its many shortcomings were accepted and lived with. Somehow, export sales were made to Honduras, Portugal and Lithuania prior to 1939. No doubt they, like the Italian Army, found they had been sold a troublesome pup.

14 Czechs and Brens

One of the new nations born from the 1919 Treaty of Versailles was Czechoslovakia, which soon set about demonstrating the inherent technical 'can do' abilities of its population. Knowing from history that sooner or later their new state would be subject to the dominance of neighbouring Germany, one of the first duties of the new nation's leaders was defence. Due to its central position in the old Austro-Hungarian Empire, Czechoslovakia found its armouries full of many and varied weapons, far too many for logistic comfort and most of them ancient. As one example, in 1920 ten different calibres of small arms ammunition were needed. Modernization was necessary, with a light machine gun as a priority.

Salesmen from all the small arms manufacturers of Europe swarmed to Prague to promote their wares, but the Czech Army was not going to be rushed into a hasty decision. A light machine gun was only one part of a major re-equipment and manufacturing programme that would demand a drastic revision of the new nation's industrial infrastructure. In the meantime, prolonged trials took place with careful assessments of every test gun's major attributes and faults. The trials took so long that a native product became ready for consideration, from the Zbrojovka Praga (Prague Armoury), designed by a team led by Václav Holek.

Starting from a belt-fed prototype, gradual development led to a Praga gas-operated light machine gun being finally selected for service in 1924. As preparing the new gun for series production would require more investment that the financially shaky Zbrojovka Praga could provide, the licence to produce its design was acquired by the state-owned Zbrojovka Brno (ZB) at Brno. Holek later moved to Brno and further work, with some input from the mighty Škoda Works at Pilsen, resulted in the 7.92mm ZB vzor 26 (vzor, or vz – model) or ZB26 (in full, the Lehky kulomet Praga vzor 26).

The ZB26 is still widely regarded as one of the best light machine guns ever devised. It was relatively light (9.6kg/21.2lb), reliable, and easy to handle and maintain. Its gas-operated mechanism was based around firing gases being tapped off from the barrel to push back a piston connected directly to a bolt carrying the separate breech block moving within cammed grooves. On the return movement the piston/block combination was so arranged that the block moved forward and upwards to lock the breech positively just before the instant of firing. Ammunition was fed from an overhead twenty-round box magazine. The mechanism operated at a steady cyclic speed of from 500 to 550rds/min using 7.92×57mm ammunition. An ingenious barrel locking system allowed rapid changing of the finned barrels, with a carrying handle doubling as the handle for a hot barrel. For the light machine-gun role the ZB26 had a folding bipod, although attachment points for tripod or other mountings were available.

Production of the ZB26 for the Czechoslovak Army began in 1927 – it eventually received 34,550. Soon after 1927 orders from elsewhere began to arrive. Holek introduced some detail changes to the bolt area on the ZB27 export model

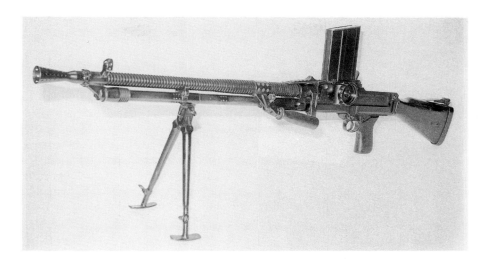

The Czechoslovak classic, the 7.92mm ZB26, rated as one of the finest light machine guns of all time.

ZB26	
Model	ZB26
Calibre	7.92mm (0.312in)
Length	1,161mm (45.75in)
Weight	9.6kg (21.3lb)
Muzzle velocity	762m/s (2,500ft/sec)
Rate of fire	500–550rds/min
Feed	20- or 30-round box

Chinese Nationalist troops manning a 7.92mm ZB26.

and more with the ZB30. To the outsider the ZB26, 27 and 30 all looked the same but there were enough internal differences between all three to preclude component swapping.

If the ZB series had any fault it was with the cost and demands of manufacture. High-quality steels were employed and almost every component had to be carefully machined from solid metal. However, while both time-consuming and expensive, the production processes did result in an extremely durable and rugged final result.

Eventually twenty-four countries used the ZB26, 27 or 30, the most important of them in the long term being the United Kingdom, of which more below. Some nations manufactured their own guns, including China (Type 26), Iran (ZB30R) and Yugoslavia (ZB30J). Japan copied the ZB26 almost direct for the 7.7mm Type 97 tank machine gun. Unintended users were the Germans who, after 1938, kept both the ZB26 and ZB30 in production at what they called the Waffenwerke Brünn AG, originally for the Waffen SS and then for more general issue. ZB guns remained in widespread use almost until the end of the twentieth century and no doubt they are still to be found.

BREN SELECTION

Mention was made in the last chapter that the British sought a Lewis Gun replacement throughout the 1920s and 1930s. Several designs were considered and at separate times a 0.303 variant of the Browning Automatic Rifle and the Vickers-Berthier were seen as likely candidates. Both were finally overtaken by the ZB27.

As a matter of policy, at least one trial example of almost every infantry weapon then available was acquired for official examination and testing, including light machine guns. Although a ZB26 was ordered under this policy, a ZB27 was sent instead. This was submitted for trials, against others, in 1930. The ZB26 emerged best on almost every score. An example chambered for the British 0.303 cartridge was requested and ZB at Brno duly obliged. The result was the first of a series of trial and developmental weapons involving both British and Czechoslovak engineers, culminating in the ZB33.

The 0.303 cartridge dictated many of the changes from the original ZB26. The propellant filling was still cordite at a time when most other nations had long adopted cleaner and more efficient nitrocellulose-based propellants. This led to a change in the gas tap-off position from its original location, close to the muzzle, to a position about halfway down the bore. This entailed a shorter piston and a revised return spring and buffer (housed in the butt), in the process reducing the cyclic fire rate to about 480rds/min, then regarded by many as the optimum for the squad fire-support role. The rimmed cartridge demanded a new curved box magazine, so that too was introduced, with the capacity extended to thirty rounds (later reduced to twenty-nine following practical experience).

Another major change was the alteration of the main body. On the original ZB26 the receiver was hinged to the butt stock assembly for interior access. On the ZB33 the butt stock group could slide to the open position horizontally. Another alteration was the removal of the barrel cooling fins. Following successful final acceptance trials, preparations were made for series production at the Royal Small Arms Factory at Enfield Lock, Middlesex. The new gun became known as the Bren, from Br – Brno and en – Enfield.

Clearly showing the changes to convert the ZB26 (top) to the British Bren Gun (below).

The official licence agreement for the UK Government to manufacture and market the Bren Gun was signed in June 1935. Production preparations were completed at Enfield Lock, with more preparations being made for the gun to be manufactured by the John Inglis Company of Toronto, Canada. The first of approximately 220,000 guns rolled off the Enfield production line in September 1937, although batches had already been delivered from Brno by then. BSA supplied components such as the bipod while many other subcontractors supplied parts. By May 1939 the initial order for 10,000 guns had been fulfilled.

TO WAR

By the time World War II commenced, all front-line units within the British Army had exchanged their Lewis Guns for Brens. When the British Expeditionary Force went to France it took Bren Guns, promptly losing all but a handful during the Battle for France and the subsequent Dunkirk evacuation. Back in the UK the entire British Army stock of Bren Guns was just over 2,300.

It was time for drastic measures. As related elsewhere, Lewis Guns were recalled to the colours until sufficient Bren Guns could be produced. Fortunately, some preparations had been made for just such an emergency. Production at Enfield Lock was expanded and the Canadian production facility was just beginning to produce guns. A group of commercial contractors centred around the Monotype & May concern had been established, although in mid-1940 they were still some months from producing hardware. Eventually the 'Monotype Group' delivered 83,438 guns.

Manufacturing short cuts were introduced. The original Mark 1 Bren had many refinements that could be left off. One was a handgrip under the butt; it was soon eliminated. A dovetail interface for an indirect fire sight was done away with and

Scots Guards manning a low-level air defence Bren Gun soon after the type was first issued.

plans to introduce a telescopic sight were dropped. Some machining operations were left off and others simplified. The bipod lost its adjustable features. Further changes introduced the Bren Mark 2, on which the original drum rear sight was replaced by a much simpler (but just as effective) leaf sight. Other Mark 2 simplifications included a non-folding carrying handle, a simpler butt stock and yet more machining short cuts. The Mark 2 demonstrated that the design could be rendered lighter and easier to manufacture, so the next stage was the shorter-barrelled Mark 3 intended for airborne and special forces. The final wartime Bren was the Mark 4 with an even shorter barrel and more metal machined away to reduce weight still further.

The John Inglis facility in Canada manufactured Brens throughout the war years, at one point diverting from 0.303 models to a 7.92mm model for China. Some 56,000 0.303 Brens were delivered to the Canadian Army alone, plus 13,189 7.92mm examples for China.

One of the more remarkable Bren production centres was at Lithgow, New South Wales, Australia. This was mainly because events back in the UK during the late 1930s were so involved that the necessary machine tools and gauges could not be spared to send to Australia. They had to be devised locally. Starting in June 1941, Lithgow had produced 17,335 guns by August 1945, most of them simplified Mark 1s or Mark 2s.

Another Bren Gun production centre at Ishapore, India, was about to become operational as the war ended. The Ishapore line did produce some

0.303 guns, with a change to 7.62 × 51mm NATO at some later undetermined date. These guns, equivalent to the UK L4A4 standard (*see below*), were still being marketed during the late 1990s.

AT WAR

The Bren Gun turned out to be one of the most successful infantry weapons of its type. Throughout the war years, and after, it proved itself to be rugged, reliable and efficient under all conditions encountered, from desert to jungle.

A light armoured vehicle was named after the Bren, the so-called Bren Gun Carrier. This was a lightly armoured and open-topped tracked vehicle

A British Army Bren Gun in action in Italy; note the spare barrel cooling off on the wall above the gun.

The Bren Gun Carrier, one of many thousands of Universal Carriers to be built.

in the Universal Carrier family. Issued at the rate of ten to an infantry battalion, the Bren Gun Carrier could carry two guns, one mounted in the front shield for forward firing and the other on a pintle. Both were likely to be carried into action and then dismounted for combat. The Carriers were manufactured by the thousand, 5,501 being produced in Australia and New Zealand alone.

Numerous alternatives to the usual folding bipod appeared. A tripod that could be converted for air defence was introduced, while more specialized air defence mountings appeared, such as the Motley, Lakeman and Gate, all the latter mounting two guns and cartwheel sights. These were almost always provided with a special 100-round drum magazine.

Infantry Bren Guns went into action handled by a crew of two. One acted as the gunner while the other carried more ammunition and a spare barrel ready for changing. For resupply, each member of the accompanying infantry squad carried two loaded magazines in their webbing pouches. The Bren Gun was rarely deployed as a sustained-fire weapon. Instead it formed the basis of an infantry squad's firepower, with bursts typically limited to three or four rounds, something made easier by the low rate of fire. A fire selection switch allowed single shots to be fired.

Bren Guns were issued to resistance organizations operating within Occupied Europe as well as with all arms of the British and Commonwealth armed forces. The massive production efforts that began in 1939–40 were eventually able to produce more than enough guns. The older makeshifts such as the Lewis Gun were gradually withdrawn and had vanished by late 1944.

NEW CALIBRES

The 0.303 Bren Gun served well throughout the Korean War and during many other post-1950 campaigns, but with the advent of NATO a spirit of standardization arrived. There was no question of retaining the old 0.303 cartridge, so when a decision was made during the early 1950s that a new 7.62 × 51mm cartridge would be adopted as the NATO standard rifle round it seemed that new weapons would be adopted as well. However, the residue of the Bren Gun mass production of the war years still remained. It made economic sense to utilize those guns, so a gradual programme of converting Bren Guns to accommodate the new 7.62mm ammunition was undertaken and continued for many years at various centres.

There were several 7.62mm Bren models, the main one being the L4A4, following a new designation system. The full range of conversions covered from L4A1 to L4A7, the latter being a prototype only. The different categories denoted

the original model used for the conversion and the necessary standard of calibre-related modification. The more widespread models, such as the L4A4, benefited from the introduction of chromed barrels that made prolonged firing possible, so each gun was issued with only one chromed barrel. A similar calibre conversion programme was carried out in India, this time at a factory at Kanpur.

The 7.62mm was not the only post-war calibre conversion. Nationalist Chinese forces in Taiwan took a 7.92mm Inglis Bren as a starting point and manufactured their M41 chambered for US 0.30-06 ammunition. Little is known of the M41 – it does not appear to have been manufactured in quantity.

The 7.62mm Brens served with the British armed forces, including the Royal Navy, for many years. They were gradually edged out following the introduction of the 7.62mm L7A2 series of general-purpose machine guns, not being finally declared obsolete by UK authorities until the late 1990s. By then it was no longer a UK front-line

Post-war Bren Gun on a field exercise, complete with Blank attachment at the muzzle.

weapon, other than as a pintle-mounted vehicle gun on self-propelled artillery or as a weapon issued to home defence units of the Territorial Army.

Bren Guns still serve on around the world, especially in India where they remain a trusted and valued weapon. Many old soldiers look back

A 7.62mm L4A4 Bren in the field supported by a soldier with a 7.62mm L1A1 rifle.

on their association with the Bren Gun almost with affection. Many serving soldiers would love to have it still.

Bren Mark 1	
Model	Bren Mark 1
Calibre	0.303in (7.7mm)
Length	1,155mm (45.5in)
Weight	9.95kg (22.12lb)
Muzzle velocity	744m/s (2,440ft/sec)
Rate of fire	480–500rds/min
Feed	29-round box

One of the first photographs issued showing an L4 series 7.62mm Bren.

15 More Czechs

By the late 1930s the Czechoslovak small arms industry was widely regarded as one of the best in the world. All manner of innovative small arms designs were produced as part of their national rearmament programme, a programme that included heavy machine guns.

During the 1920s the standard Czechoslovak heavy machine gun was the water-cooled Schwarzlose 7.92mm vz 7/24 (also known as the vz Š), an elderly and cumbersome weapon converted from the original Austrian 8mm at the Zbrojovka Janeček in Nusle, Prague. That concern also placed the Schwarzlose back into production as the 7.92mm vz 24 until 1931 in order to gain some form of standardization and meet required equipment levels. The Czechoslovak armed forces had 7,140 of these guns in 1938, even though it had long been considered that something better was needed.

Václav Holek duly obliged once again. He took the operating system from the light ZB26, modified it for belt feed, and added a heavy, air-cooled 7.92mm barrel in a finned jacket. To add strength to the locking system the barrel could move to the rear while locked to the breech block by lugs after firing. After a short travel the locking mechanism disengaged and the barrel returned to its usual position. One unusual feature was two selectable rates of fire, 550 or 750rds/min. Another was the method of cocking (charging) the gun, carried out by moving the firing grips backwards and forwards.

The factory designation was ZB53, but as the Army adopted it in 1937 it became widely known as the vz 37 or, in full, Těžký Kulemet vzor 37.

The vz 37 proved to be an excellent weapon that was widely exported, as well as being manufactured in quantity for the Czechoslovak Army. The infantry version usually appeared on a tripod mounting, although there were special variants for incorporation into the Sudetenland fortification (with an even heavier barrel), and another for armoured vehicles. By September 1938 the Czech Army had received about 700 guns for armoured vehicle installations, 1,464 for fortifications and 1,300 for the infantry.

After 1938, the Germans reintroduced the vz 37 into production in late 1940. Between then and the end of 1942, 5,161 examples were delivered to the Waffen SS, although it eventually became a standard issue, the 7.92mm MG 37(t), throughout the Wehrmacht. Production started again in 1944 when a further 1,250 guns were completed. The German-owned guns were widely deployed, hundreds still in the armoured mountings originally intended for the Sudetenland defences, along the Atlantic Wall. Many of the light PzKpfw 38(t) tanks manufactured in Czechoslovakia for the Germans were armed with the MG 37(t).

Post-war production of the vz 37 continued until 1951. The export total from 1936 onwards was over 14,000 to at least ten nations. In 1948 Israel received at least 900.

BESA

Having adopted the ZB33 as the Bren Gun (*see* previous chapter), the British Army was impressed by Czechoslovak products, so in late 1936, when

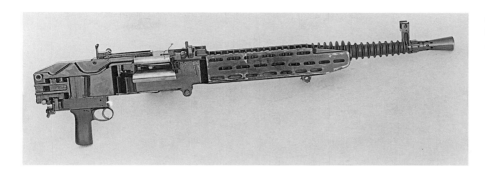

Starting point, the Czechoslovak 7.92mm ZB53.

End result, the Birmingham Small Arms 7.92mm Besa.

it came to consideration of an air-cooled machine gun to arm future British tanks, the Army once again turned to Brno and the ZB53. This time there was no consideration given to conversions to British ammunition or other niceties. War was imminent so, as the Royal Armoured Corps had its own supply infrastructure, it was decided to produce 7.92 × 57mm ammunition in the UK.

BSA obtained a licence to manufacture the ZB53. As its Small Heath facility in Birmingham was already bursting at the seams, a new factory to manufacture the gun was built at Redditch. A further four factories were later opened at Leicester. Firm War Office orders arrived in April 1938, after which the programme moved into the pre-production phase, only for BSA to receive an unwelcome shock.

As with the ZB26, the Zbrojovka Brno design was demanding to manufacture, requiring extensive and time-consuming machining to low tolerances. BSA technicians therefore had to undertake an engineering redesign of the ZB53 before they could pronounce it ready for mass production on the scale considered necessary. To differentiate

their revised model it was named the Besa. It was May 1940 before a production rate of 200 a month was reached, but thereafter the quantities soared, assisted on the Mark 3 model by the omission of the dual firing rate feature. The final production total was 59,322, with enhancement modifications still being introduced as late as 1952.

The BSA output was for tank and armoured car installations only, although the gun could be dismounted on to a bipod for ground use. The Besa supplemented and then replaced the old Vickers Guns as the secondary armament of

Besa	
Model	Besa
Calibre	7.92mm (0.315in)
Length	1,110mm (43.7in)
Weight	21.15kg (47lb)
Muzzle velocity	823m/s (2,700ft/sec)
Rate of fire	450 or 700–750rds/min
Feed	225-round belt

British armoured vehicles and as such they served on for many years after 1945, only gradually being replaced, in their turn, by Brownings from 1958 onwards.

ZB60

When Holek joined the Zbrojovka Brno in 1928 the original intention was that he could concentrate on heavy calibre automatic weapons. Due to his diversion to the ZB53 programme the large-calibre project was set aside, only to re-emerge in 1938 as the 15mm ZB60. This was really a scaled-up ZB53 intended as a multi-purpose weapon, with potential applications varying from anti-tank to aircraft installations. In the event, the main application was as an armoured vehicle gun.

The original intention was that the ZB60 would fire explosive 15 × 103mm projectiles, ostensibly against aircraft targets, but trials demonstrated that their performance was 'disappointing'. Yet the Czechoslovak Army remained interested in the ZB60, placing orders with the understanding that the gun would be manufactured at a new Zbrojovka Brno facility at Vsetín. Deliveries were delayed by a series of lucrative export orders from Greece and Yugoslavia. While some of the export orders were fulfilled, the bulk of the Zbrojovka Vsetín output was destined to be for Germany, where the gun was adopted as the 15mm FlaMG 39, an air defence model that was not widely adopted other than for static defences.

However, the main ZB60 export destination was the UK. It formed part of the same BSA licensing transactions that led to the 7.92mm Besa, although, unlike that Besa, the ZB60 was adopted direct with few alterations, becoming the 15mm Besa. Once again, BSA prepared a production line at Redditch, the intention being that the ZB60 would be an armoured-vehicle gun. As things turned out, priority had to be given to the 7.92mm Besa, the 15mm Besa finding few applications. Production was limited to 3,218, most of them apparently never issued. The main applica-

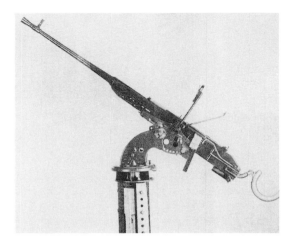

Side-on view of the 15mm ZB60 heavy machine gun mounted for the low-level air defence role.

tion was on the Light Tank Mark VIC, a type withdrawn by 1942.

AIRCRAFT GUNS

Although the Czechoslovak air arm had to rely on imported aircraft guns during the 1920s, the Czech determination on national self-reliance in defence matters led to Vickers and Lewis Guns being rechambered for 7.92 × 57mm ammunition at the Česká Zbrojovka at Strakonice. From that exercise emerged the 7.92mm vz 28, an interim model before the final selection of the 7.92mm vz 30, first produced at Strakonice and then at Uherský Brod. The vz 30 was a recoil-operated weapon along Browning short-recoil lines, with ammunition feed from an overhead Lewis-pattern drum or a belt. Fixed and flexible mountings appeared, with production running at such a rate from 1936 onwards that it exceeded the required monthly acceptance figure. By March 1938 the vz 30 was the standard Czechoslovak aircraft gun, with 4,825 delivered by then, although this total was still a long way from the planned requirement

level. By 1938 it was appreciated that heavier calibres than 7.92mm would soon be required to arm aircraft, one reason for the development of the 15mm ZB60, which, ultimately, arrived too late.

POST-1945

After 1945 Czechoslovakia attempted to return to its pre-1938 position of pre-eminence in small arms production. Although many important products were to follow, the former happy state was not fully achieved. It was not for want of trying, although many promising Czechoslovak projects were crushed by Soviet dictates.

One concerned small arms ammunition. The advantages of the German 7.92 × 33mm *kurz* (short) intermediate power cartridge and its associated *Sturmgewehr* were recognized by Czechoslovak ammunition designers who introduced their own 7.62 × 45mm Model 1952 round. This was slightly more powerful than the equivalent

Soviet 7.62 × 39mm Model 1943 cartridge, enabling better all-round performance from weapons no heavier than the Soviet assault rifles and squad machine guns then entering service. To cut a long story short, the Czechoslovaks were forced to abandon their cartridge in favour of the Soviet Model 1943, but not before weapons to fire the Model 1952 round had been introduced.

One of these was the 7.62mm vz 52 light machine gun (factory designation ZB501), another product from Václav Holek and Zbrojovka Brno. In over-simplified terms, this was a ZB26 updated to utilize ammunition fed from either a twenty-five-round box magazine or a 100-round belt. The rapid-change barrel system was retained and a novel 'half moon' trigger introduced, with the top segment for single shots and automatic fire from the bottom. Cocking the gun was achieved by moving the pistol grip backwards and forwards. The main portion of the receiver required extensive and careful machining, although some savings were introduced by placing the receiver inside a stamped steel body. Machining tolerances

*The belt-fed 7.62mm
vz 52 – note the two-
segment trigger.*

were so tight that even slight contamination by dirt or dust could cause problems.

The vz 52 was adopted by the Czech armed forces but it was not a great success. No overseas orders resulted. Experience showed that the combined magazine and belt-feed arrangement, although efficient and compact, was really too complicated for a general issue weapon. It also became appreciated there was no overwhelming tactical reason for having such a capability. The vz 52 gradually faded away, although not before Soviet dictates had resulted in the vz 52/57, a vz 52 converted to chamber the Soviet 7.62mm Model 1943 cartridge. The enforced acceptance of the vz 52/57 brought the Czechoslovak small arms industry back into line with the rest of the Warsaw Pact.

vz 52	
Model	vz 52
Calibre	7.62mm (0.30in)
Length	1,041mm (41in)
Weight	7.96kg (17.55lb)
Muzzle velocity	746m/s (2,450ft/sec)
Rate of fire	1,150rds/min
Feed	30-round box or 100-round belt

RACHOT

Post-1945 concentration on the ZB53 and vz 52 disguised the fact that the general-purpose machine gun (GPMG) concept and market potential was appreciated rather late in the day by the Czechoslovak arms industry. At one stage the national requirement for a heavy machine gun was met by local production of the Soviet 7.92mm SGM, but that came nowhere near any GPMG standard. By the time attentions were directed to the GPMG, Czechoslovak industry had been left behind.

The late 1950s witnessed the establishment at Brno of a local small arms 'think tank' and design house known originally as the Výzkumně vývojový ústav, later renamed as Prototypa Brno. When the designers turned their attentions to a GPMG the result was the 7.62mm vz 59, a remarkably efficient gun forming what may have been the last in the line of machine guns based on the ZB53, augmented with the belt feed of the vz 52. In true GPMG style, the air-cooled vz 59 can be provided with a bipod and light barrel for the light machine-gun role, or a tripod and heavy barrel for the sustained-fire role. Conversion from one role to the other remains rapid and easy. The vz 59 fires the Soviet full power 7.62 × 54R rifle cartridge in 250-round belts or a fifty-round belt carried in a side-mounted box. One unusual option is a ×4 telescopic sight.

The 7.62mm vz 68 Rachot configured as a light machine gun, complete with optical sight.

Following acceptance trials the vz 59 was placed in production at the Zbrojovka Vsetín, with 37,222 being produced between 1960 and 1975. Almost all were for the Czechoslovak armed forces, for the vz 59 appeared after most other nations had already made their GPMG selections, while the Soviet ammunition had few attractions outside the Warsaw Pact. In an attempt to find more widespread acceptance, in 1968 a variant chambered for 7.62 × 51mm NATO ammunition appeared, named the Model 59N. There were still no takers. It seemed as though all commercial interest in the vz 59 series had lapsed.

However, during the late 1990s a new marketing drive commenced. The 7.62mm NATO Model 59N was reintroduced as the Model 68 Rachot and promoted at numerous defence equipment exhibitions. The original vz 59 also remains on offer. In a further attempt to extend the appeal of the Model 68 Rachot a tank turret version

vz 59	
Model	vz 59
Calibre	7.62mm (0.30in)
Length	1,220mm (48in)
Weight	*c.* 9.6kg (19lb)
Muzzle velocity	823m/s (2,700ft/sec)
Rate of fire	750rds/min
Feed	50-round belt

appeared, the Rachot-T, again in both 7.62mm Soviet (TK95) and NATO (TK98) ammunition forms. Both tank guns can be converted for the infantry role by the introduction of a conversion kit.

No known sales have yet been made of the 'export' models, although the original vz 59 serves on with the now separated Czech and Slovak armed forces.

16 German Innovations

Mention has been made elsewhere of the German General Staff post-1918 analyses of the events of the World War I years. As would be expected, the results were thorough and detailed. From them came no end of indications as to how the next war should be fought, with the emphasis on tactics and the equipment needed.

That the machine gun would be part of this scrutiny was a certainty. Despite the lethal successes of the German Army's machine-gun units, even before 1918 it was considered that the weapons they had were unsatisfactory. The sMG08 was too heavy while the leMG08/15 was a cumbersome makeshift. While it was appreciated that the division between light and heavy machine guns would remain, technical advances were such that it seemed possible somehow to amalgamate the two into one base weapon. It was forecast that a machine gun light enough to be carried into action, and fired, by one soldier was essential, yet it was also forecast that the same weapon should be capable of sustained fire from heavy mountings. Changing between the two roles without difficulty was required, so provision for such changes had to be integrated into the design. It would be a bonus if that same weapon could be adapted for vehicle and aircraft mountings.

Thus the theory of the general-purpose machine gun (GPMG) was born, promising all the advantages of manufacturing and logistic commonality, easier training and adaptability. Early on in the studies it became apparent that to save weight the weapon would need an air-cooled barrel and that a quick-change barrel would be essential for sustained-fire missions.

It was one thing to prepare theoretical specifications, but during the 1920s things were so difficult for the new German Reichswehr that any further developments had to be low key and concealed from the gaze of Versailles Treaty monitors. In addition, funds were short. But there was something to start with.

EARLY ATTEMPTS

Before 1918 the GPMG concept had been forecast by the 7.92mm MG16 from the State Arsenal at Erfurt, which produced what was termed as an *Einheitsmaschinengewehr*, or Universal Machine Gun. The intention was that the Maxim-based MG16 would be much lighter than the sMG08 yet would still be capable of being more comfortable to handle and more accurate then the leMG08/15. Provision was made for both bipod and tripod mountings. Water-cooling was retained but with a reduced-capacity jacket to save weight.

Although the MG16 promised much it appeared at the wrong time. After 1914, German industry was already overburdened, so to divert manufacturing facilities to any new weapon, no matter how promising, was not possible. The MG16 remained at the prototype stage and was forgotten after 1918. Yet it had sown the seeds for the eventual GPMG.

It was mentioned in Chapter 10 that an air-cooled version of the Dreyse machine gun, the 7.92mm leMG18, had appeared in 1918 but arrived too late to make any impact. As it embodied some of the features of the projected GPMG, the Dreyse

A Dreyse 7.92mm leMG13 crew undergoing training in the low-level air defence role.

was used as the basis for one of the first projects undertaken by Rheinmetall-Borsig AG (usually known simply as Rheinmetall) at Sommerda. With Louis Stange leading a design team, the 7.92mm leMG13 appeared during the late 1920s, the 13 (1913) being a subterfuge to hide the post-1918 development from Treaty investigators. As with the leMG18, the leMG13 had an air-cooled barrel. It introduced the seventy-five-round saddle drum magazine that was to become a German GPMG trademark; a horizontal twenty-five-round box magazine was an alternative. The leMG13 was officially adopted in 1932, although numbers had been around for some years by then.

Although the leMG13 was better than nothing it was not what the German staff planners had

The long barrel and large conical muzzle-flash hider indicate this is a 7.92mm leMG13 – the butt stock is folded to reduce the carrying length.

envisaged. Apart from being a long and awkward weapon that, at 11.43kg (25.2lb), was really too heavy for the light machine-gun role, the air-cooled barrel could not be changed rapidly.

The leMG13 was therefore issued as a training weapon. When more suitable alternatives became available the German Army's leMG13s were sold, the bulk going to Portugal where they remained in service (in Angola) until the early 1980s. However, the Germans retained some leMG13s, for they appeared in the Channel Islands in mid-1940.

MG30

Louis Stange of Rheinmetall was instrumental in the next step towards the GPMG. To conceal its weapon development activities from the ubiquitous Treaty monitors, Rheinmetall acquired an 'off-shore' facility that became the Waffenfabrik Solothurn AG, at Solothurn in Switzerland. The first result of this arrangement was the 7.92mm MG29 that soon evolved into the Solothurn S-2-200, the MG30.

At first sight the recoil-operated MG30 appeared to meet the GPMG specifications. It had a rapid barrel change system (although it required the use of an insulated glove for hot barrel handling), but the ammunition feed was limited to a side-mounted twenty-five-round box magazine. As the MG30 had a cyclic fire rate of 800rds/min

(high fire rates were to become another German machine gun trademark) this involved frequent magazine replacements. The German Army therefore turned the MG30 down.

Some orders for the MG30 did result, known customers including El Salvador, Austria and Hungary. Austria took about 5,000, only for them to enter German service after all, following the Austrian Anschluss of 1938. As they were chambered for non-standard 8 × 56mm Solothurn ammunition, the Austrian loot was used only for training or limited second-line duties.

To complete the story that began with the Solothurn MG30, the Luftwaffe did procure a slightly modified variant, the 7.92mm MG15. It was retained as the standard Luftwaffe flexible or fixed aircraft gun for many years. From the MG15 came the MG17 for wing or nose installations. Examples of the MG15 were licence-produced in Japan for the Japanese Army (Type 98) and Navy (Type 1).

Both the MG15 and MG17 fired standard 7.92 × 57mm rifle-calibre ammunition, regarded as too light for air warfare by 1943. Both were gradually withdrawn from the airborne role and, provided with rudimentary bipods, butt stocks and seventy-five-round saddle magazines, distributed as field service expedients, first to Luftwaffe ground troops and later to Wehrmacht units. MG17s, being remotely fired weapons, usually ended up on multiple air defence mountings.

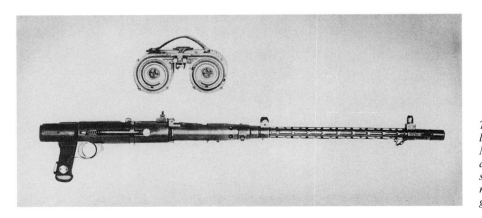

The slim and elegant lines of the 7.92mm MG15, originally an aircraft gun but subsequently modified for the ground role.

MG34

Once again, Louis Stange and Rheinmetall were involved in the next GPMG step, this time to the 7.92mm MG34. The MG30 was the development source, with Stange carrying over two of that weapon's most original features. One was an all-in-line layout from the muzzle to the butt that not only looked efficient but distributed some of the recoil forces on the firer's shoulder more evenly. The other was a 'half-moon' trigger where pressing the upper segment produced single shots, automatic fire resulting from pressing the lower segment. The main Rheinmetall contribution was an efficient and adaptable ammunition feed mechanism over the receiver.

However, Rheinmetall did not have things all its own way, as there were others in the hunt for the GPMG contract. Also active was the Mauser-Werke AG, which had observed the potential of the MG30 and introduced a rotary interrupted thread bolt head actuated by cams for firm locking

at the instant of firing. This locking system was so attractive that it was integrated with the updated Rheinmetall design. The result, the 7.92mm MG34, was officially adopted in 1936.

The 7.92mm MG34 turned out to be a superb GPMG, meeting all the specifications laid down over a decade previously. Three types of ammunition feed were possible: a side-mounted drum containing a fifty-round metal link belt; a seventy-five-round saddle drum (as introduced on the leMG13); or 250-round belts. Three basic mountings were available: a folding bipod usually retained in place under the barrel; a heavy and complex tripod on to which the entire MG34 could be placed; and a lighter tripod. Other accessories proliferated, including twin mountings for low-level air defence, numerous vehicle mountings, flexible, coaxial and armoured gimbal mountings for armoured and other vehicles, and special mountings for fortifications. Telescopic and dial sights were introduced for the tripod applications, as were numerous niceties such as

Western Desert, May 1942, with South African troops turning a captured 7.92mm MG34 against enemy aircraft.

The four main 7.92mm MG34 models: A, the standard production MG34; B, an attempt to make a simpler MG34; C, the short MG34S; D, the MG34/41, produced for troop trials only.

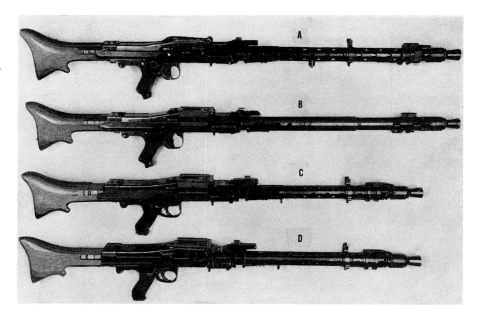

tubular spare-barrel containers, special ammunition carriers, and dust covers to mention but a few. Some of the accessories, such as the heavy tripod that contained over 200 components or the heavy fortification mountings used along the Atlantic Wall, cost far more than the MG34 itself.

The MG34 could therefore appear in many forms. The usual crew was two or three, all carrying spare barrels, ammunition and various special tools. The cyclic fire rate was 800rds/min, so sustained fire entailed changing the barrel every 250 or so rounds, the insulated glove of the MG30 being carried over. The gun itself weighed 11kg (24.3lb), while the heavy tripod added a further 23.6kg (52lb). The latter allowed indirect fire out to 3,500m (3,829yd).

The MG34 proved to be highly popular with its users and was reluctantly respected by all who had to suffer its ministrations. But behind all this success was a snag. The MG34 had been introduced at a time when the German future seemed rosy, but after 1939 that outlook had altered. By then the MG34 was too good.

The MG34 embodied all the old gunsmithing qualities of close manufacturing tolerances, fine finishing and high-quality raw materials. The result, although reliable and durable, became too expensive, complicated and time-consuming to manufacture under war conditions. Demand constantly outstripped supply, even though several production centres other than the Mauser-Werke were established. It proved impossible to keep pace with combat losses and the constant expansion of the German forces. A simpler, easier to produce solution was required.

Eventually the MG42 emerged, but in order to maintain existing MG34 lines in production, simplified variants with shorter barrels were proposed. To keep things as simple as possible, there was provision for automatic fire only, while the fire rate increased to 1,200rds/min. There were two main variants in this category. The MG34S was not adopted, although its successor, the MG34/41, was placed into production as a stopgap in case problems arose with the MG42. They did not, so only 1,705 MG34/41s were made.

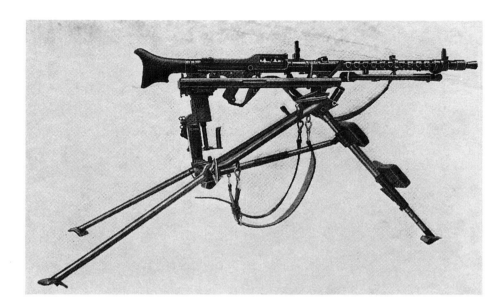

German service manual illustration of a tripod-mounted 7.92mm MG34.

A 7.92mm MG34 configured as a light machine gun, Eastern Front, Winter 1941.

MG34	
Model	MG34
Calibre	7.92mm (0.312in)
Length	1,219mm (48in)
Weight (bipod)	11.5kg (26.7lb)
Muzzle velocity	755m/s (2,480ft/sec)
Rate of fire	800–900rds/min
Feed	75-round drum

Total MG34 production between 1939 and 1945 reached 354,020, with examples still being manufactured at the Waffenfabrik Brünn when the war ended. Luftwaffe ground troops and the Kriegsmarine also received the type. For some reason, a batch of MG34s was sold to Portugal in 1944, a time when they were sorely needed back home. More were passed to Bulgaria.

After the end in 1945 the MG34 did not fade away. Many armies, such as the reborn Czechoslovak and Israeli, took over remaining examples, while worn but still serviceable examples continued to turn up in Africa and the Far East until the late 1980s at least. The Balkan campaigns of the late 1990s unearthed more MG34s, although they were probably pre-1945 war relics.

MG42

By 1941 demands for machine guns had reached such a pitch that an alternative to the MG34 had to be considered. Fortunately for the German armed forces the solution was already close to hand, although from an unusual source.

In 1939 an engineering concern not normally involved with defence matters, the Johannus Grossfuss Metall- und Locierwaren Fabrik of Döbeln in Thuringia, introduced an experimental machine gun that came to the attention of the Mauser-Werke. It became the 7.92mm MG39/41, incorporating numerous design features adapted from Czechoslovak, Polish and Italian sources. The main Grossfuss contribution came from one

Doctor Grunow, who was primarily an industrial engineer rather than a gunmaker. As a result of his background, Grunow was able to dispense with many of the long-established design and manufacturing constraints adopted by conventional gunsmiths. In place of the usual careful machining processes and the employment of the finest raw materials available, Grunow adopted manufacturing processes involving cheap and simple sheet steel stampings, pressings, welds and rivets. Where possible, mouldings were used in place of machined or forged items. These measures alone were able to speed production and reduce manufacturing costs significantly, although they were not solely responsible for the success of what was to come.

In 1940 the Grossfuss concern acquired an experimental Polish machine gun with an innovative roller locking method. In simple terms the bolt had rollers that, at the instant of firing, locked into grooves cut into the receiver walls. Following MG34 practice, a muzzle attachment contained an expansion chamber that allowed propellant gases to push back the locked barrel and bolt until cams allowed the rollers to move out of their locking grooves. By then the chamber pressures had fallen to a safe level so the bolt could separate from the barrel and commence its rearward travel for the extraction and reloading cycles, the barrel, as usual, returning to its former position.

The advantage of this locking system was that it contained few moving parts and demanded a minimum of machining during manufacture. It also provided the weapon with a prodigious rate of fire, the cyclic rate being from 1,200 to 1,500 rds/min, depending on environmental and ammunition-batch variations. Barrel climb, a usual by-product of fast automatic fire, was reduced to a minimum by a special muzzle brake attachment from 1943 onwards. The necessary barrel changes were greatly assisted by the introduction of an ingenious side lever arrangement that disconnected the barrel from the receiver and presented it for removal from the right-hand side of the barrel jacket. A further lever movement

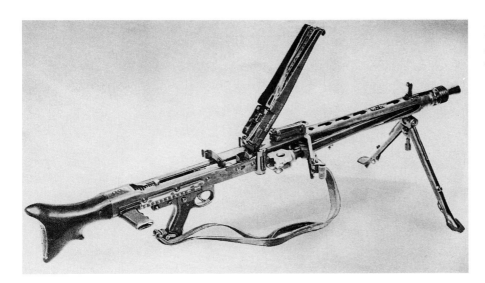

The 7.92mm MG42 with the top cover open ready to insert an ammunition belt.

reinserted the fresh barrel, the entire operation taking but seconds.

Fire rates have always been a constant source of discussion among machine-gun designers and users. Before the 1930s most considered that 500 rds/min was the optimum, but the demands of low-level air defence gradually increased the rate to about 800rds/min. By introducing an even higher rate the gun that was to become the MG42 was producing twenty to twenty-five rounds every second. Even at that time, many observers regarded this rate as wasteful of ammunition while creating premature barrel wear and component stress. In response, the firepower of the MG42 produced extreme results, even from short bursts – there was no single shot facility. Bullets could be sprayed all over and around a target within fractions of a second. Allied troops came to respect the MG42.

In 1941 the Mauser-Werke added its own refinements to the Grossfuss/Grunow MG39/41, the result being accepted as the 7.92mm MG42 and placed into production at the Mauser-Werke. Other MG34 production centres switched to the MG42, and the Grossfuss concern obtained a contract for all its pains. Between them, these

centres managed to deliver 414,964 MG42s to the Wehrmacht, 2,402 to the Kriegsmarine and 4,014 to the Luftwaffe. For once, the Waffen SS was at the end of the queue, receiving just 225. These totals were remarkable by any standard, and especially under war conditions, but the MG42 was designed for rapid and easy production at a time when such assets were badly needed. Almost all MG42 output went direct to front-line formations. Few second-line units ever saw an MG42.

A similar range of combat accessories was provided for the MG42, even more than for the MG34, but there was only one ammunition feed mode, namely fifty-round belts that could be connected to form a 250-round belt. There was no provision for the MG34 magazines, the entire feed system being so efficient that it was later adopted by numerous post-war machine guns. As a general rule, accessories for the MG42 were usually simpler and less finely finished than those for the MG34, to the point where there was little interchangability between the two families. MG42 accessories included an enlarged trigger guard for when wearing thick gloves, and a device with a periscopic sight to permit firing from behind parapets. As before, tank and vehicle mountings

The MG42 was converted for many roles by the application of a series of special accessories – this example was for firing over parapets.

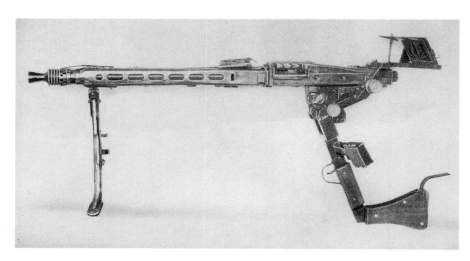

appeared. One bonus for the front-line soldier was that the MG42, at 10.6kg (23.4lb), was marginally lighter than the MG34.

No doubt German soldiers were aghast when they first saw the MG42, as its lack of finish was not what they had come to expect. However, once the MG42 was used in action any reservations were swiftly forgotten, for the MG42 proved to be reliable, rugged and lethal under the most extreme conditions. Many authorities still regard the MG42 as one of the finest GPMG designs ever to appear. Unfortunately for the German war machine, MG42 demands remained far higher

than German industry could meet, something not helped by the huge combat losses that grew and grew from 1943 onwards.

By 1945 the MG42 was still the subject of attempts to make it even simpler to manufacturer, some late production examples being delivered still in the 'bare metal' state. Development work also continued, one result being the 7.92mm MG45 with a fire rate of at least 1,500rds/min. In 1945 this was still at the prototype stage, so at that time it made no impact on proceedings and vanished into the maelstrom of post-1945 Europe. During 1961 the outlines of the MG45 reappeared

The Swiss 7.62mm SIG 710-3 as a light machine gun.

in a revised form as the Swiss 7.62mm SIG 710-3. The SIG gun attracted a great deal of technical interest but also attracted zero sales and was withdrawn into obscurity.

The US Army was so impressed by the MG42 that it attempted to copy the gun during 1943. Introducing provisions to handle the US 0.30-06 cartridge resulted in conversion errors being introduced to degrade performance so severely that the project was abandoned, the resultant T24 passing into oblivion.

STILL GOING

As might be expected, the MG42 was too good a gun simply to fade away after 1945. Austria and France (among others) took over as many examples as possible to arm their post-war armed forces. War-year MG42s still appear in odd corners of the globe, from Lebanon to Vietnam.

By the late 1950s the European political situation had reached the point where Germany had to be rearmed as a partial counter to the Soviet threat. When it came to the selection of a machine gun for the emergent Bundeswehr there was no discussion. It had to be the MG42, so production in Germany commenced once again. This time the main producer was Rheinmetall Industrie GmbH, the successor to the old Rheinmetall-Borsig AG. Initial production was in 7.92 × 57mm calibre to

get production lines going using surviving tools – this became the Bundeswehr MG1, but it was only a stopgap until everything was ready for future guns to be manufactured to fire 7.62 × 51mm NATO ammunition. To Rheinmetall the 7.62mm gun was the MG42/59 but to the Bundeswehr it was the MG1A1, the Rheinmetall designation being retained for export sales, for the MG42/59 was sold in considerable numbers. MG42/59s were sold to Spain and Austria, while a batch of those sold to Italy are in the process of being converted to take 5.56 × 45mm ammunition.

The MG1A1 and MG42/59 both had a far higher standard of finish than the war-year guns. In addition, their barrels were chromed to extend the intervals between barrel changes. Variants soon appeared, the MG1A2 being able to accommodate different ammunition belt links. The MG1A3 introduced some production changes and a revised muzzle attachment, while the MG1A4 and MG1A5 were special fixed installation models. 7.92mm MG42s brought up to 7.62mm standard became the MG2.

The 7.62mm MG3 was the final production model based on the M1A3, but was able to utilize both US and German belt links. A programme to update all previous models to MG3 was undertaken for the Bundeswehr. One addition on the MG3 is a 100-round belt drum for the assault role. The MG3S was licence-produced in Spain at one time. One further variant is the MG3A1 mounted

The final MG42, the Rhinmetall 7.62mm MG3 – this example was licence-produced in Pakistan.

on tanks, such as the Leopard series, and some other armoured vehicles.

Rheinmetall no longer produces the 7.62mm MG3 series, but licence production continues elsewhere, notably by Pakistan, Turkey, Greece and Iran. All these countries offer their products for export sales, so the MG42 seems likely to remain around for decades to come.

OTHER MG42s

A fair proportion of the MG42s that remain in use throughout the Balkans are locally produced clones known as the Zastava M53 or SARAC M3, still chambered for locally manufactured 7.92 × 57mm ammunition and complete with accessories identical to those produced in Germany before 1945.

In 1951 the Swiss Waffenfabrik Bern (written as w + f Bern) produced a 7.5mm machine gun, the M51. The M51 has many affiliations with the MG42, but, being Swiss, is far better made and weighs 4kg (8.8lb) more. The Swiss decided that the MG42 locking rollers were better replaced by sprung flaps, but the M51, acquired only by the Swiss armed forces, is otherwise similar to

the MG42. The 7.5mm M83 is a variant of the M51 developed for the Swiss Army's Leopard 2 tanks.

One other non-German weapon with MG42 connections is the Spanish CETME (now General Dynamics Santa Barbara) 5.56mm Ameli. Despite Spanish protestations to the contrary this is essentially an MG42 or MG42/59 scaled down for 5.56 × 45mm ammunition and weighing only 5.3kg (11.7lb). Unlike the full-scale MG42 and although it can be fired from a tripod, the Ameli has always been regarded as a light squad fire-support weapon, with an optional disposal box containing a 100-round ammunition belt. Ammunition can also be fed in 200-round belts.

At one stage the Ameli seemed to have a bright future, but the only takers have been the Spanish armed forces. However, the Ameli is still marketed for possible sales.

Bearing a distinct visual resemblance to the MG42, the 5.56mm Ameli is now a General Dynamics Santa Barbara product.

MG42	
Model	MG42
Calibre	7.92mm (0.312in)
Length	1,220mm (48in)
Weight (bipod)	11.5kg (26.7lb)
Muzzle velocity	755m/s (2,480ft/sec)
Rate of fire	>1,500rds/min
Feed	50-round belt

17 The Soviet War Story

The Soviet Union's Great Patriotic War of 1941 to 1945 was fought using three machine-gun types. They were the 12.7mm DShK-38, the Maxim 7.62mm PM1910 and the light DP. After 1943 these guns were joined by the SG43. Rigid standardization made it possible to keep churning out machine guns in thousands to supply the expanding Red Army and to replace the enormous losses seemingly unavoidable on the Eastern Front. There was a price to be paid for this manufacturing capability. The PM1910 had to be kept in being, even though it was obvious its day had passed.

SG43

The search for a Maxim replacement began during the late 1920s. Vasiliy Degtyarev suggested a variant of the 7.62mm DP allied to a belt-feed mechanism derived by Georgy Shpagin. Prototypes were under test by 1934, but thereafter development proceeded at a hesitant pace as it was the time of the Terror Trials when any display of personal initiative was inadvisable. It was not until 1939 that the Degtyarev design was finally decreed as suitable for service as the DS1939. By then the gun had acquired several technical novelties when compared to the DP base. Two rates of fire were possible, 600 or 1,200rds/min, and the finned air-cooled barrel could be rapidly replaced using the carrying handle.

The DS1939 was rushed into production only for serious defects to appear. Ammunition feed jams were numerous, the dual fire-rate feature proved troublesome and structural weaknesses became apparent. Investigations revealed the troubles were too inherent to be solved other than by introducing extensive changes, so in June 1941 the DS1939 was withdrawn from production and manufacturing priority reverted to the old PM1910.

That left the Soviets with a machine gun already regarded as obsolete by being too heavy and complicated to manufacture, but during the early months of the German invasion it was the PM1910 en masse or nothing. Some improvement work was attempted on the DS1939, although by the time it was once again ready for testing something better had appeared.

That something was based around a simple specification. Any new gun had to be as easy to manufacture as the DP while being as reliable as the PM1910. Work had commenced on such a possibility during 1940 when Petr Goryunov teamed with his brother Mikhail and Vasiliy Voronkov to design an experimental, gas-operated light machine gun, the 7.62mm GVG. The GVG embodied many of the mass-production features, such as metal stampings and welds, that were later to govern small arms design, yet it was durable and reliable. Unfortunately, the GVG appeared just at the wrong time. The German invasion of 1941 meant it had to be sidelined in favour of more urgent activities.

But the GVG idea did not entirely vanish. The PM1910 replacement requirement remained, so, despite the Soviet Union fighting for its very survival, some diversion of effort and resources was allotted to machine-gun development. Using the GVG as a basis, the overall design was considerably strengthened by Goryunov, one example being that the stamped GVG receiver was replaced by a stronger machined component. Another was the installation of a very heavy air-cooled barrel with a rapid-change mechanism. To prolong barrel life and reduce barrel changing to a minimum, the barrel interior was chromed. A gas operating system similar to that of the Czechoslovak ZB26 was adopted, but with the breech block locking sideways into a recess in the receiver body.

By March 1943 a batch of fifty guns was field-tested, resulting in some modifications before final acceptance as the 7.62mm Stankovity Pulemet Sistemi Goryunova obr 1943 or SG43. To save time it was decided to adapt the Sokolov wheeled mounting, complete with shield, from the PM1910. Mass production commenced almost immediately at several centres, the accumulated total by late 1944 being about 74,000. In time, a SG43B model appeared with some minor changes to the barrel locking system and dust covers over the feed mechanism apertures.

The rush to get the SG43 into service meant that some non-critical defects inevitably became apparent under field conditions, although while the war lasted they had to be endured. In action the SG43 proved robust and able to withstand the worst possible combat and environmental conditions to keep on firing for as long as required. Although the combined gun and mounting weighed 40.7kg (89.7lb), that still made it much lighter and more mobile than the PM1910.

As soon as the Great Patriotic War was over the SG43 was revised in several aspects, such as the barrel gaining longitudinal flutes and the cocking handle moving from under the spade grips to the right-hand side of the receiver. The old Sokolov shield was discarded, while the rest of the wheeled mounting was revised to allow it to be rapidly configured for low-level air defence. After these post-1945 modifications the SG43 became the SG43M, more widely known as the SGM.

An SGMT appeared for coaxial tank applications while licence production began in Czecho-

Man-handling a SG43 up an incline, never a light task.

slovakia and Poland. Another manufacturer was Hungary where, during the 1960s, the state arsenal considerably modified the SGM to become a GPMG, the KGK; less than 1,000 were made. The China North Industries (Norinco) concern still offers an SGM copy, the 7.62mm Type 57, while another manufacturer still able to churn out the SGM is the Egyptian Maadi Company for Engineering Industries, by whom it is marketed as the 7.62mm Asswan.

SGM production in the Soviet Union ceased during 1961, being replaced by the PK (*see* Chapter 19). As the SGM remains available from the above-mentioned sources it is likely to be encountered almost anywhere for many years to come. It remains a reliable and effective machine gun.

SG43	
Model	SG43
Calibre	7.62mm (0.30in)
Length	1,120mm (44.1in)
Weight	40.7kg (89.7lb)
Muzzle velocity	863m/s (2,830ft/sec)
Rate of fire	500–640rds/min
Feed	50-round belt

DSHK-38

It was not until the mid-1920s that the Soviet Union displayed any interest in heavy machine guns and then only by noting trends elsewhere. The Soviet notion of a large-calibre machine gun was originally directed mainly to low-level air defence and to save time a British Vickers 0.50in (12.7mm) was adopted for early gun studies. Once again, the name of Vasiliy Degtyarev was connected with the design programme, his first submission, the 12.7mm DK, appearing in 1930. It was basically a scaled up and beefed up 7.62mm DP. The DK was tested in opposition to a local copy of a 12.7mm Dreyse gun but both were found wanting. The cyclic rate of fire for both was considered too low and practical firing on the DK was rendered still slower by the need to change the thirty-round drum magazines at frequent intervals.

Degtyarev got around both drawbacks by making some internal changes to increase the fire rate and adding a fifty-round belt-feed mechanism devised by Georgy Shpagin. The result was the 12.7mm DShK-38, but the ammunition had changed as well.

The Vickers round selected for trials was regarded as too low-powered, so a new 12.7 × 107mm cartridge having enhanced muzzle energy was developed. In time this 12.7mm ammunition family expanded into several natures, including armour-piercing (AP), armour-piercing incendiary (API) and high-explosive incendiary (HEI). So successful was this 12.7mm ammunition family that it remains in widespread service to this day, with new natures still appearing.

To return to the DShK-38, production began in late 1939, the first examples reaching the troops in mid-1940. The gun was placed on a heavy wheeled mounting designed by Ivan Kolesnikov, so arranged that the towing trail unfolded into a tripod. A shield was available as an option, as was a wheeled Sokolov mounting. As with the DP, the mechanism was gas-operated, one notable

The 12.7mm Degtyarev DShK-38 on its ground mounting.

A 12.7mm Degtyarev DShK-38 on an air defence mounting.

DShK-38 recognition feature being the heavy fixed and finned barrel with a large, distinctive muzzle brake. The rate of fire was a cyclic 525 rds/min.

One other feature of the DShK-38 was the weight, mainly due to the solid construction techniques involved. As with other Soviet machine guns it was much heavier than its contemporaries – 37.2kg (82lb) for the gun alone, never mind the mounting. War production of the DShK-38 appears to have been relatively modest compared to other Soviet weapons, as by early 1944 the Red Army had just 8,442. By that time the DShK-38 had been adopted as a tank turret gun, one of the first models so armed being the IS-2 heavy tank.

Production of the DShK-38 did not cease after 1945, but continued involving a modified feed. The original DShK-38 ammunition feed was based on a rotary system, the rounds being extracted from the belt as a rotary sprocket turned. This was a complicated process that could cause jams unless great care was taken by the loader in the two-man team. It was also difficult to manufacture, so even before the war ended a new ammunition feed had been proposed. This was a more conventional, simpler shuttle-feed system, resulting in the DShK-38/46. This model remained in production in the Soviet Union until the early 1970s, in the process becoming one of the machine-gun mainstays of the old Warsaw Pact armed forces.

Production of the DShK-38/46 in the former Soviet Union may have ceased but the gun remains available from elsewhere. The Chinese Norinco concern continues to market its 12.7mm Type 54, a clone of the DShK-38/46, together with the Type 59, the tank version. In addition, the Pakistan Ordnance Factories manufacture the Type 54 under Chinese licence. Other current manufacturers include Iran and Romania.

The DShK-38/46 remains a formidable land and air defence weapon to this day, constituting for many years the nearest Eastern Bloc equivalent to the formidable Browning M2 HB.

DShK38	
Model	DShK38
Calibre	12.7mm (0.50in)
Length	1,602mm (62.3in)
Weight	33.3kg (73.5lb)
Muzzle velocity	843m/s (2,765ft/sec)
Rate of fire	525rds/min
Feed	50-round belt

POST-WAR HEAVY

At this point it would be as well to mention one further heavy machine gun that had wartime origins, the 14.5mm KPV. The Soviets were enthusiastic proponents of the anti-tank rifle long after most other nations had discarded the concept. Their 14.5mm PTRD-41 and PTRS-41 anti-tank rifles remained in service until well after 1945, by then being retained as anti-materiel rifles as much as anti-armour weapons. As early as 1942 a proposal was forwarded for some form of anti-

tank machine gun firing the armour-piercing, high-velocity 14.5 × 114mm cartridge, but the project had to be allotted a low priority until 1944.

During 1944 one Semen Vladimirov drew up plans for what was to become the belt-fed 14.5mm KPV. The Vladimirov design was uncomplicated, employing an innovative short-recoil locking mechanism. Locking involved a rotary action into the barrel sleeve for firing, with unlocking under the control of an accelerating lever. This principle, allied with a cylindrical body, made manufacture relatively simple, something made even easier by the introduction of numerous metal stampings, rivets and welds.

At first the KPV's weight (49.1kg (108.3lb) for the gun alone) limited applications to armoured vehicle and air defence mountings, one of the most successful of the latter being the ZPU-4 carrying four KPV guns. (A Chinese copy is the Norinco 14.5mm Type 56, the Type 75-1 having a single barrel, the Type 58 having two.) The armoured vehicle variant, at one time the main armament for Soviet-era reconnaissance and other light armoured vehicles, is the KPVT. Now little

Four 14.5mm KPV heavy machine guns on a ZPU-4 air defence mounting.

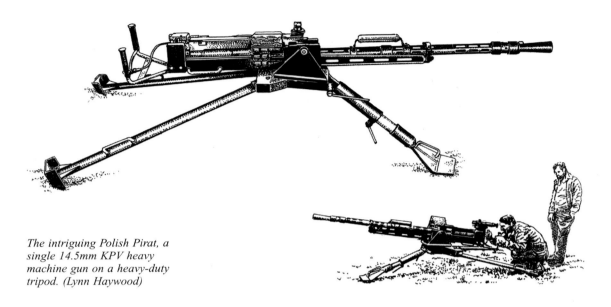

The intriguing Polish Pirat, a single 14.5mm KPV heavy machine gun on a heavy-duty tripod. (Lynn Haywood)

known is the ZGU-1 single gun air defence unit intended to be broken down for back-packing by mountain troops and involving a slightly modified KPV gun. By the time the ZGU-1 carriage was finally accepted in 1968 the standard KPV gun was no longer in production, so the few ZGU-1s produced were exported to North Vietnam.

For infantry deployment the KPV was placed on a wheeled carriage, which, after the wheels were removed, became a heavy tripod. In this form the gun was known as the 14.5mm PKP, first appearing in 1955. However, the PKP does not appear to have been produced in quantity. It required a light truck for towing, a vehicle that might be better used for other more powerful loads, so the PVP faded away. However, the KPV infantry mounting has not completely vanished for in 1993 a Polish Army workshop at Zurawica produced the 14.5mm Pirat on a heavy, purpose-built tripod. As far as is known the Polish Pirat remains a prototype.

The 14.5mm KPV is no longer in production within Russia. It remains available from Bulgaria, China, North Korea and Romania. There is no sign of the KPV vanishing from the scene, as it remains a formidable low-level air defence weapon. Its high-velocity (988m/s) projectiles remain more than capable of knocking out light armoured vehicles or field fortifications, delivering accurate fire out to well over 2,000m (2,188yd).

KPV	
Model	KPV
Calibre	14.5mm (0.57in)
Length	2,002mm (78.8in)
Weight	48.97kg (108lb)
Muzzle velocity	988m/s (3,250ft/sec)
Rate of fire	600rds/min
Feed	100-round belt

18 FN's GPMG

After 1945, as after 1918, the military world was awash with machine guns. Almost everywhere, machine-gun production had peaked just before hostilities ceased, leaving all armies with sufficient armaments to keep them going for years. Yet changes were afoot. The 'one gun fits all' GPMG concept pioneered by the MG34 and MG42 had indicated that no technical challenges remained. All future rifle-calibre machine guns were to be GPMGs. Even so, the surplus of the war years ensured that no new designs were introduced for well over a decade. When they did start to appear, one of the most successful of them all was the product of Ernest Vervier, a design engineer of FN in Herstal, Belgium.

MAG

As outlined in Chapter 11, FN was deeply involved in BAR production and development, both before 1940 and after 1945. Vervier simply took the well understood BAR gas-operating mechanism, beefed it up and added the ammunition feed of the MG42. The result was the Mitrailleuse d'Appui Generale, usually known simply as the MAG, or MAG-58 from its year of introduction. Many apply the term Mitrailleuse à Gaz as an alternative. Whatever its title, the MAG incorporated many design detail innovations from the war years, such as the use of chrome plating for the bore and other areas subject to hard wear, and introduced a few of Vervier's own.

What Vervier did not adopt were the war-year production methods. Rapid production measures involving pressings, welds and rivets were simply ignored. In their place Vervier ensured that almost every part of the MAG is painstakingly machined from solid metal. This may mean that the MAG remains somewhat heavy (10.85kg/24lb) when employed on a bipod for the light machine gun role, but this is more than balanced by the extremes of durability and reliability that the MAG can display under extreme combat and environmental conditions.

For an air-cooled machine gun, a tripod-mounted MAG can still produce prodigious amounts of sustained fire, even if it cannot quite manage the performances of the old water-cooled guns. The MAG has a rapid-change barrel system combined with a stout carrying handle. Ammunition feed is from linked fifty-round belts. The cyclic fire rate can be from 650 to 1,000rds/min according to the setting of the gas valve at the tap-off point in the barrel and also to ammunition and environmental variations.

Although the MAG is a truly universal machine gun, FN market it in three main models. The Model 60-20 is the infantry gun with over fifteen variations possible according to mountings, typical of these being with the butt stock removed when the gun is on a tripod. The Model 60-30 is for installations inside underwing aircraft pods or pods on helicopters. The Model 60-40 is for co-axial mountings on armoured vehicles. The Models 60-30 and 60-40 differ from the infantry Model 60-20 in having remote firing arrangements and no provision for sights. Components can still be freely interchanged between all three base models, while the Model 60-40 can be reconfigured for

FN's GPMG

The FN 7.62mm MAG, seen here on a tripod but with the butt stock still in place.

A familiar sight all around the world, the FN 7.62mm MAG.

*A twin-gun 7.62mm MAG mounting specifically developed for the Belgian Minerva
Land Rover.*

tripod mountings by using an adaptor kit. The
three base models have since been joined by the
MAG58P, a model with spade grips for vehicle or
aircraft applications. (There was a Model 60-10
'jungle' model with a shorter barrel and butt stock,
but there were no takers so that model was withdrawn.)

Apart from the various models there are two
distinct MAG categories. These relate to the
ammunition feed – one category is intended for
disintegrating (M13) metal link belts, while the
other is for non-disintegrating belts. The two categories are not interchangeable.

MAG mounting possibilities are legion. The
infantry models usually remain with a selection of

bipods, tripods, or tripod 'softmounts'. The latter
carry the gun on a buffer spring cradle that
absorbs most of the recoil stresses, assisting the
aim to remain constant throughout prolonged
bursts. Also available are armoured-vehicle roof
mountings, vehicle single or twin ring and pintle
mountings, naval mountings, helicopter door
mountings, and so on.

Many of these mounting variations have come
about by the sheer widespread distribution of the
MAG. Sweden was the first to adopt the gun, firing
the then standard Swedish 6.5 × 55mm ammunition. Thereafter the gun has been available only
for 7.62 × 51mm NATO ammunition – even the
Swedes converted their guns to 7.62mm from

1962 onwards. After Sweden, the MAG was adopted by over seventy countries, remaining in licence production with five. The licence producers are Agentina, Egypt, India, the UK and the USA. (A sixth manufacturer, Singapore, does not have a licence.) The MAG remains available from FN Herstal, the corporate successor to FN.

Of this list two deserve special mention as their MAGs differ in several respects from the Belgian original. The widest differences come from the UK.

L7 SERIES

By 1957 the British Army began actively seeking a replacement for its well-loved but increasingly obsolescent Vickers Gun. The MAG arrived on the scene just at the right time for, after a series of trials, it was adopted as the British Army's first GPMG. Production in the UK began in 1963 at the Royal Small Arms Factory at Enfield Lock although, as with the earlier Bren, the British insisted on their own modifications to suit their requirements exactly, and on design changes to suit local manufacturing methods and processes. As a result, 'British' MAGs may appear to be identical to the original MAG but detail differences abound.

The first British MAG was the 7.62mm L7A1, soon supplanted by the modified L7A2 that remains the main infantry version. From the L7A2 a string of variants appeared, all of them developed within the UK but retaining the original Belgian outlines. For the record, a brief outline of these variants is provided here to give an indication of how one basic GPMG design can be adapted in many ways.

* L8A1 and L8A2 – tank coaxial guns, the L8A1 for the now withdrawn Chieftain, the L8A2 for the Challenger series.

A British Army 7.62mm L7A2 GPMG complete with indirect fire sight.

A British Army Supacat all-terrain load carrier armed with a 7.62mm L7A2 GPMG.

* L19A1 – a heavy barrel infantry model to minimize the need for barrel changing.
* L20A1 and L20A2 – for helicopter pods.
* L37A1 – a mix of L7 and L8 components to form the armament for light armoured vehicles such as the FV432 and Saxon APCs.
* L37A2 – a revised L37A1 for the Challenger tank series.
* L41A1 – inert training model of the L8A1.
* L43A1 – ranging machine gun for the now withdrawn Scorpion reconnaissance vehicle.
* L45A1 – inert training model of the L37A1.
* L46A1 – inert training model of the L7A2.
* L120 – a L7A2 converted for the low-level air defence role.

Production at Enfield Lock ceased in 1987, just before that facility closed, but the L7A2 series remains available from Manroy Engineering of Beckley, East Sussex. Manroy is still busy manufacturing the many variants of the L7A2, plus associated spares and accessories such as mountings.

Within the British Army the tactical employment of the L7A2 has become varied of late. When the L86A1 Light Support Weapon (*see* Chapter 21) appeared, the L7A2 was largely withdrawn from the squad fire-support role, but in recent years, following combat experience in the Balkans, it is making something of a comeback at the expense of the L86A1. The 'British' MAG will be around for many years yet, especially with the Commonwealth nations to whom the L7A2 series was sold.

US M240

In 1979 the US Army ordered an initial 16,417 FN MAG Model 60-40 7.62mm coaxial machine guns for its M60 tanks, replacing the ageing 0.30 M1919A4 Brownings and interim 7.62mm M73 machine guns employed until then. The FN guns became the M240D, used not only on M60 tanks but also with the later M1 Abrams. The M240C is a variant with right- or left-hand feed to suit installations in M2/M3 Bradley IFVs. Both weapons were provided with adaptor kits for ground-mounted purposes, although it seems they were rarely so employed.

The US Marine Corps, also M60 tank users, came to recognize that the M240D was phenomenally reliable. Rounds fired between failures could reach well over 26,000, far more than any other known equivalent weapon. They came to note that the only way an M240D could stop firing was by releasing the trigger or if the ammunition ran out. Other MAG owners had reached the same conclusions many years before.

The Marines therefore acquired some surplus M240D guns from the Army for permanent conversion for the ground role as the M240G, a gun almost identical to the original MAG although an aluminium tripod was developed to replace the original steel version. The first M240G was issued during 1994. So successful was the M240G in its 'new' role that the US Army took note, as it also wanted something reliable to replace the outdated M60. The result was a series of comparative trials until the M240G emerged as being far ahead of anything else likely to be considered, so the M240B was ordered into production in May 1997. The M240B differs from the Marines' M240G by the addition of a substantial forward handguard, but otherwise the two guns are similar.

M240 series production in the USA is still in progress at an FN Herstal subsidiary, FN Manufacturing Inc. of Columbia, South Carolina.

MAG	
Model	MAG
Calibre	7.62mm (0.30in)
Length	1,250mm (49.2in)
Weight	10.15kg (22.25lb)
Muzzle velocity	853m/s (2,800ft/sec)
Rate of fire	>1,000rds/min
Feed	belt

Total production there by 1986 had reached 22,775, many of the guns for foreign military sales. M240 series contracts were all due for completion by the end of 2002, but production continues. The intention was to have around 12,000 M240 series guns available for US service until 2012, although that total may still emerge as an underestimate.

M240 series guns have undergone some modifications to suit US requirements. One is the provision of a hydraulic buffer to reduce the cyclic rate from about 750rds/min to 630rds/min, reducing fire dispersion in the process. The modification also reduces the gun weight by 1.36kg. Other planned changes include revised vehicle mountings and the provision of MIL-STD-1913 Picatinny mounting rails to permit the rapid and easy installation of various optical and night sights.

The M240 series, as with the original FN MAG, still has a long way to go.

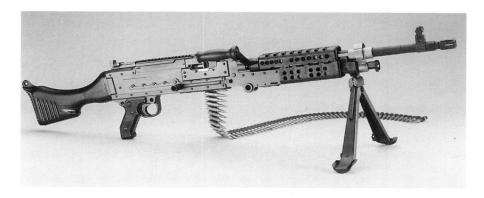

The US Army's 7.62mm M240B GPMG.

19 GPMGs and Heavies

So successful was the FN MAG GPMG that it gained a sizeable chunk of the available market. As a result, relatively few equivalent models appeared as serious rivals, the only exceptions being from a few nations where local circumstances dictated the adoption of a local product. The two main rivals to the MAG were the US M60 and the Soviet/Russian PK.

M60

As mentioned briefly in Chapter 16, the Americans were very impressed by the German MG42, but it was not the only German weapon they admired. They also studied the Rheinmetall/ Krieghoff 7.92mm FallschirmjägerGewehr 42 (FG42), an early assault rifle developed for Luftwaffe airborne troops. The FG42 was something of a design study in getting a quart into a pint pot. Although meant to be a fully automatic assault rifle, it fired full power 7.92 × 57mm ammunition in place of the lower powered 7.92 × 33mm *kurz* (short) ammunition adopted for Wehrmacht assault rifles. The FG42, employing a much-modified Lewis Gun gas-operated mechanism, suffered somewhat by the compromises in weight and performance that had to be accepted, but its operating mechanism became the subject of close study by US ordnance personnel.

It seemed sensible to combine the commendable features from the MG42 with those of the FG42. After much development work the two were combined in the 7.62mm T161E3, the final test model before type classification during 1957

as the 7.62mm M60. In effect, the MG42 belt-feed mechanism was allied with a strengthened piston and bolt from the FG42, but by the time the two disparate systems had been successfully amalgamated a great deal of lengthy and intensive work had to be completed. Even then the M60 suffered from a series of 'teething troubles' before settling down as an accepted weapon.

Initial development work dated back to 1945 when the initial T44 experimental model appeared, chambered for 0.30-06 ammunition. Much of the protracted work relating to the subsequent T52, and then the sub-variants of the T161, was carried out by the Bridge Tool and Die Manufacturing Company of Philadephia and the Inland Manufacturing Division of General Motors of Dayton, Ohio. The subsequent production contract, awarded during the early 1960s, went to the Maremont Manufacturing Company of Saco, Maine. (Maremont later became Saco Defense, before becoming part of General Dynamics Weapon Systems during the late 1990s.)

The M60 became well accepted by the US Army even though it displayed shortcomings compared to other designs then available. It remains a somewhat bulky GPMG with a flimsy carrying handle, awkward lines and a weight of 11.1kg (24.5lb). The barrel is chromed, which is just as well as a 'rapid' barrel change involves removing the bipod and gas cylinder as well – the bipod forms the only means of handling a hot barrel, other than an asbestos glove. Many observers regard the cramped rearsight arrangements as unsatisfactory, although as a zeroed foresight is removed with a barrel change, consistent

*A 7.62mm M60
machine gun on a
vehicle mounting.*

*A US Army soldier unloading
his kit, including an M60,
from a truck.*

An Australian soldier on guard with a 7.62mm M60 machine gun.

accuracy cannot be degraded much further. There is also the problem that removing and replacing the rotating bolt assembly is not a task for the technically illiterate.

Having said all that, the M60 gained high regard from US military personnel who valued its reliability, smooth operation and cyclic fire rate of 500 to 650rds/min. Having a 100-round belt carried in a side-mounted box was also seen as a useful asset. Its main combat sphere became South-East Asia and it was procured by Australia (mainly for commonality reasons during the Vietnam campaigns), South Korea and Taiwan. The M60 was licence-produced in Taiwan, although the Taiwanese version, the Type 57, has a finned barrel.

Apart from the M60 infantry model, several other versions appeared. The M60C was a stockless, remotely fired variant for external mounting on helicopters. Also for helicopters, as well as vessel or vehicle applications, is the M60D with spade grips. The M60E2 was another remotely

fired variant intended as a coaxial gun for armoured vehicles.

Then came two models intended to make the M60 more user-friendly. The first was the M60E3 with the weight reduced to 8.8kg (19.4lb). Two M60E3 barrels are available, a short, light barrel for the assault role, for which a foregrip is provided, and a longer, heavier barrel for more prolonged fire. The carrying handle was transferred to the barrel to assist barrel changing and the bipod is secured to the receiver, making it unnecessary to remove it along with the barrel. Various other details were introduced. It is possible to convert standard M60s to M60E3 standard by using a kit. The M60E3 is in service with the US Marine Corps.

The M60E4, also procured for the US Marine Corps, is the latest M60 variant, introduced to extend further the user-friendliness of the series. Three main variants are available, a light machine gun with a short barrel, a vehicle-mounted gun, and a coaxial gun for armoured vehicles, both the

M60	
Model	M60
Calibre	7.62mm (0.30in)
Length	1,105mm (43.5in)
Weight	10.4kg (23lb)
Muzzle velocity	853m/s (2,800ft/sec)
Rate of fire	500–650rds/min
Feed	belt

latter having longer and heavier barrels. Improvements introduced on the M60E4 include a strengthened bipod, improvements to the belt-feed system, MIL-STD-1913 Picatinny rails for installing various optical or night sights, and changes to the trigger group assembly. Once again, standard M60s can be uprated to M60E4 standard by a conversion kit.

The M60 series is being phased out of front-line service with the US Army in favour of the M240B. Production and support for the M60 series remains available from US Ordnance Inc. of Sparks, Nevada.

ENTER KALASHNIKOV

By the mid-1950s Soviet military authorities were noting GPMG events then occurring elsewhere and became determined not to be left behind at a time when a replacement was needed for the SG43 and RP-46. Their main problem was that the only suitable full-power rifle-calibre cartridge in their inventory was the rimmed 7.62 × 54R dating from 1895. As a general rule, rimmed cartridges for machine guns demand more complicated feeding and handling arrangements than rimless cases. By the late 1950s rimless cases had been adopted almost universally. Yet the Soviet Union retained the cartridge originally intended for Mosin-Nagant bolt-action rifles. This was mainly because production facilities were still well established for churning out rounds by the million. Developing any new cartridge and its production facilities required time and resources, so the 7.62 × 54R had to be retained and there is still no sign of any alternative.

The design bureau established around Mikhail Kalashnikov at the Izmash concern at Izhevsk was responsible for what was to become the 7.62mm

A 7.62mm PK on a tripod mounting – note the 5.56mm RPK in the foreground.

PK (Pulemet Kalashnikov). It appears that to save time and development effort, the Kalashnikov team adopted a mixture of well-tried components and ideas from other weapons. As might be expected, the PK rotating bolt was the same as that used in the highly successful Kalashnikov AK-47 series assault rifles. The barrel change mechanism of the SGM was adopted, the trigger group came from the Degtyarev RPD (*see* following chapter), while driving the feed mechanism using the gas piston was carried over from the Czech vz 52. Getting all these bits and pieces to work together was no doubt a challenge, but it meant the gun was that much easier and cheaper to manufacture using existing facilities and by the ability to incorporate numerous stamped or cast components. By contrast, a similar competing weapon designed by Grigory Nikitin and Yury Sokolov was more demanding in manufacturing resources. It was therefore the PK that was adopted in 1961.

The PK has remained in production ever since. Despite all its various bits and pieces the PK works extremely well. It is easy to handle and maintain and it operates reliably under harsh conditions. It weighs only 9kg (20lb) and its latest associated tripod, designed by Leonid Stepanov, is not only lighter (7.5kg/16.5lb) than the gun it carries but is relatively easy to manufacture and can be adapted as an air defence mounting. One refinement of the Stepanov tripod is an ammunition box secured to one leg, enabling the gun to be carried into action already loaded and ready for action. Boxes are available for 100-, 200- or 250-round belts.

In true GPMG style the PK can also be fired from a bipod. This is the configuration for the PK proper. When the tripod is utilized the gun becomes the PKS. These two are far from being the only PK derivatives to have been produced. A short checklist outlining these follows:

* PK – bipod mounting, fluted barrel, for direct infantry fire support.
* PKS – tripod mounting, fluted barrel, for the heavy machine gun role.
* PKT – remotely fired coaxial weapon for armoured vehicle installations, with a longer barrel.
* PKD – a hybrid produced by Kaspex of Kazakhstan by combining the PKT with an added pistol grip and a tubular butt stock to act as a slightly heavier (10.9kg/24lb) form of PK.
* PKM – a lighter version of the PK introduced in 1969, featuring a lighter unfluted barrel and reduced weight (8.4kg/18.5lb).
* PKMS – tripod-mounted equivalent of the PKM; this variant introduced the Stepanov tripod.
* PKMSN – a PKMS fitted with a night sight.
* PKB – with spade grips and butterfly trigger.

The 7.62mm 6P41 Pecheneg, a revised PK with a heavy fixed barrel and the bipod mounted at the muzzle to enhance accuracy and deliver long bursts of fire.

PK	
Model	PK
Calibre	7.62mm (0.30in)
Length	1,193mm (47in)
Weight	8.9kg (19.75lb)
Muzzle velocity	822m/s (2,700ft/sec)
Rate of fire	650rds/min
Feed	belt

* 6P41 Pecheneg – a revised PK with a heavy fixed barrel and the bipod mounted at the muzzle to enhance accuracy and deliver long bursts of fire.

More variants result from licensed manufacture. Apart from Kazakhstan, PK series manufacturers include Bulgaria, China (Type 80), Poland, Romania and the former Yugoslavia (M84). Among the models produced within Poland is the Grom (Thunder), having a pintle mounting for naval or fixed installations.

SS77

Of the current generation of GPMGs, none can claim a more unusual provenance than the South African Vektor 7.62mm SS77. It was born at a time when United Nation sanctions against the old South African regime were at their most effective. Before sanctions were imposed the South African Defence Force had adopted the FN 7.62mm MAG. They found the gun was really too heavy for most infantry deployments and something lighter was needed, although the 7.62mm calibre had to be retained as 5.56mm could not deliver the long-range accuracy required by operational units.

Unable to obtain new materiel from abroad, the South Africans were forced to develop their own. Starting in 1977 two Armscor engineers named Smith and Soregi (hence SS77) had managed to combine features from several machine-gun designs, along with some new ideas, into a new weapon. For instance, the locking mechanism of the Soviet SG43 was adopted while the trigger group was taken from the Bren, as was the barrel-change process.

The combination of features from other designs has resulted in an outstanding GPMG even if, at 9.6kg (21.2lb), the SS77 is slightly heavier than many of its contemporaries. Some of this weight has been added as strengthening, as a constant South African requirement has always been reliability combined with durability. Most infantry operations of that period were carried out at great distances from any base and under the worst

The South African Vektor 7.62mm SS77 machine gun.

Two 7.62mm SS77 machine guns combined on a vehicle roof mounting.

conditions imaginable, so the gun had to be able to keep on firing when needed. The SS77 can do that well, while remaining simple to operate and handle. An indication of that simplicity can be seen in there being no method of adjusting the amount of operating gas tapped from the barrel. Early models had an adjustable regulator, but it was later omitted to simplify matters.

Ammunition is fed from factory sealed, 200-round plastic boxes clipped under the gun, one practical detail being that the gunner can see how many rounds are left at any time. A flexible pouch holding 100 rounds is an alternative. To reduce overall length the butt stock can be folded to one side of the receiver or even removed. A folding bipod is a fixture, though the SS77 can be mounted on a tripod or on a series of vehicle and other mountings. One extreme is the Rattler, a four-gun combination for firing from helicopter side or rear hatches.

Although the SS77 was ready for trials by the end of 1977, it was not until 1986 that it entered service as the L9. The interval was imposed not for technical reasons but by the intrusion of more

urgent priorities as the operational situation along South Africa's borders changed. Once matters had settled down production commenced at the Vektor facility at Lyttleton, not far from Pretoria, one export sale being made to Kuwait.

One unusual feature of the 7.62mm SS77 is that it can be converted to a 5.56mm Mini SS light machine gun by using a conversion kit. The Mini SS was announced in 1994, with the empty weight reduced to 8.3kg (18.3lb). Ammunition is fed in 100-round belts stowed in a pouch known as an assault pack. An optical sight is optional.

SS77	
Model	SS77
Calibre	7.62mm (0.30in)
Length	1,160mm (45.7in)
Weight	9.6kg (21.16lb)
Muzzle velocity	840m/s (2,756ft/sec)
Rate of fire	600–900rds/min
Feed	belt

A French AAT 52 7.62mm machine gun in the light machine gun configuration; this machine gun was also produced in 7.5mm calibre.

FRENCH ATTEMPT

After 1945 the French Army had mainly US and British weaponry plus captured German small arms, but was determined to produce its own GPMG, mainly for reasons of self-sufficiency. The result was the AAT 52 firing the 7.5 × 54mm cartridge introduced back in 1929 (*see* Chapter 13), the AAT 52 standing for Arme Automatique Transformable mle 52. In their enthusiasm for producing something purely French, the design engineers at the Manufacture Nationale d'Armes

de Châtelleraut managed to devise a most unusual operating system based around a delayed blow-back action, but perhaps the most unusual aspect of this was the method of aiding extraction.

The chamber of the AAT 52 has longitudinal grooves machined along the chamber, so arranged that after firing some of the propellant gases seep along the grooves to help to prevent the case from sticking to the side walls. Breech opening is delayed for an instant by a lever mechanism on one section of the heavy bolt, which prevents the head section of the bolt moving until the lever has

An early production 7.5mm AAT 52 machine gun on a prototype air defence tripod.

completed its short travel. This system can work well enough, although even slight ammunition variations can cause extraction or worse problems. The extraction action is somewhat rapid and violent to the extent that cases can be deformed, despite the measures taken to prevent such troubles. Somehow the principle seems to work, although many design engineers have been critical of its efficiency.

Be that as it may, the AAT 52 went into production, first at Châtellerault and then at Tulle. With the NATO adoption of the 7.62 × 51mm round, production switched to the new calibre and existing guns were gradually converted as well. In this form the gun is known as the N AAT.

Despite being intended as a GPMG the gun served mainly as a light machine gun, known to the French armed forces as the mle NF-1. In this form the gun has a bipod plus an optional adjustable height monopod under the shoulder stock to add firing stability, although it is often omitted. Changing the NF-1 barrel is something of an art, for once the hot barrel is released the bipod goes with it and there is no means of supporting the gun or handling the barrel. Another shortcoming is that loaded ammunition belts have to be left flapping around as no provision for any form of container feed seems to have been considered, other than on a few vehicle mountings.

Having outlined some of the deficiencies of the AAT series compared to other weapons, it has to be said that the gun is relatively easy to manufacture, compact and easy to handle. Two barrel weights are available, although only the lighter seems to have been used on any scale. Numerous fixed and flexible mountings have appeared.

The 7.62mm N AAT is no longer marketed by Giat Industries, the successor to the various state-owned arsenals, and it appears that most in-service weapons have either been withdrawn or relegated to the reserves. Export sales were delivered to nations as disparate as the Seychelles and Iraq, as well as to former French colonies in Africa.

N AAT	
Model	N AAT
Calibre	7.62mm (0.30in)
Length	1,080mm (42.52in)
Weight	10.6kg (23.37lb)
Muzzle velocity	830m/s (2,723ft/sec)
Rate of fire	900rds/min
Feed	100-round belt

H&K

The Heckler & Koch GmbH GPMGs do not at first sight appear to qualify as such. Being based on the H&K assault rifles and sharing the same roller locking mechanism, they at first seem to be heavy barrelled rifles, something reinforced by many components in both the rifle and machine-gun categories being interchangeable. The first H&K GPMG was the now-discontinued HK21, with the option of a twenty-round magazine, eighty-round drum, or linked belt feed. It was also available in both 7.62 and 5.56mm calibres.

What moved the HK21 into the GPMG bracket was the provision of a belt feed and a rapid barrel-change system. When required, the HK21 can be mounted on a tripod and used to deliver sustained fire for extended periods, although, as with so many current guns in the same category, the pauses between bursts should be made as extended as possible. Weapons such as the HK21 simply cannot produce the sustained fire of the old water-cooled guns. The roller locking system involved is a variant of that intended for the German 1945 MG45 (*see* Chapter 16), but further refined at the Heckler & Koch Oberndorf works. Licensed production was carried out in Portugal.

The HK21 is no longer manufactured as it was replaced by the HK21A1, available in belt feed 7.62mm form only. Numerous H&K accessories such as a heavy tripod remain available. Many export sales were made, with licence production this time taking place in Greece and the UK, the

*The Heckler & Koch
7.62mm HK21
GPMG in the
bipod-mounted
configuration.*

latter for exports to Kenya, Sri Lanka, Sudan and
Nigeria.

H&K now concentrates its marketing efforts on
two models that are basically similar, apart from
the calibre. They are the 7.62mm HK21E and the
5.56mm HK23E, both based on the HK21A1.
Improvements include a longer heavy barrel, an
extended barrel housing providing a longer sight
radius and thus enhanced accuracy, a three-round
burst limiter and a quiet method of closing the
bolt. One unusual accessory on any GPMG is the
fixed 'assault' foregrip under the forward handguard. As with the HK21A1, ammunition feed is
limited to belt feed only.

HK21A1	
Model	HK21A1
Calibre	7.62mm (0.30in)
Length	1,030mm (40.55in)
Weight	8.3kg (18.3lb)
Muzzle velocity	800m/s (2,625ft/sec)
Rate of fire	900rds/min
Feed	belt

*This universal air defence mounting was
developed by the US Ramo concern for a
variety of machine guns, including the
Heckler & Koch 7.62mm HK21.*

Based as they are on assault rifles, the H&K GPMGs lack the attractions of the purpose-built models, yet they remain highly effective, reliable and tough guns.

HEAVY 1

Although it cannot be regarded as anything like a GPMG, the NSV-12.7 is mentioned here. By the late 1960s the 12.7mm DShK-38/46 heavy machine gun, good as it was, was getting long in the tooth. Three designers, Grigory Nikitin, Yury Sokolov and Vladimir Volkov, were instructed to combine and design a replacement.

The result was the NSV-12.7, a gas-operated gun that not only proved to be simpler and lighter than its predecessor, but has an enhanced rate of fire (700–800rds/min). It also allows a smaller amount of propellant fumes to escape to cause problems within confined spaces. It is also easier to manufacture, requires fewer raw materials and is highly adaptable. The design was accepted in 1972 and has remained in production ever since.

At least three main production centres were established during the Soviet period. One is at Uralsk in Kazakhstan, now an independent state so this centre currently acts as an independent producer. The Russian centres are at Tula and Viatskie Poliany.

Despite all its advantages the NSV-12.7 remains a hefty load requiring a team of five to backpack the gun and its ammunition for the ground-based heavy fire support role. The gun, by itself, weighs 25kg (55lb), while a single fifty-round belt of 12.7 × 107mm ammunition weighs 7.7kg (17lb). The usual infantry tripod, the 6T7, weighs in at about 16kg (35.3lb).

One novelty devised for the gun is a three-part breech block. At the instant of firing all three parts are in line for locking. Only when the breech block carrier commences its rearward travel under tapped-off propellant gas pressure do the three sub-blocks move out of line, allowing one to assist in ejecting the spent case. On the loading stroke another sub-block guides the next round into the chamber and the three components then move once again into line. The action of the breech

The bulk of a 12.7mm NSV heavy machine gun, complete with optical sight.

block carrier also provides the drive motion for the feed system.

As the NSV-12.7 has an effective combat range of 2,000m (2,188yd) an optical sight is available, although iron sights calibrated to the same range are fixtures. Unusual on such a heavy gun is the provision of a simple butt stock to assist aiming.

Night sights are involved with the NSV-12.7 N3 and N4. A single gun may also be placed on a special 6U6 air defence mounting, often referred to as the ZPU-NSV. Twin guns feature with the Utes-M light naval vessel air defence turret mounting. For this mounting the ability of the NSV-12.7 to feed ammunition from either the left or right is a definite asset. There is a special tank coaxial or roof-mounted model known as the NSVT-12.7. Yet another variant is intended for mounting in fortification embrasures.

As with most other machine guns from both the Soviet and more recent Russian periods, gradual improvement of the NSV-12.7 has been undertaken. One result is the NSVP-12.7 with a multi-port muzzle brake and a 'softmount' tripod, both measures intended to attenuate recoil forces and improve accuracy. Another development has been the Kord, about which little has yet been released. It is known that the Kord is a product of the Degtyarev Plant JSC at Kovrov. Changes appear to have been introduced to the trigger system, while the barrel looks heavier and sports a multi-baffle muzzle brake. Licence production of the NVS-12.7 has been established in Bulgaria, India (NSVT-12.7), Poland, Ukraine (NSVT-12.7) and the former Yugoslavia, although production by the latter is probably now complete.

HEAVY 2

Over its long and successful life many attempts have been made to improve or replace the Browning 0.50/12.7mm M2 heavy machine gun. To date, the only result has been the replacement of old M2s by new M2s. Nothing yet devised has come anywhere near displaying enough advantages over the M2 to justify its replacement, although that has not stopped people from trying.

One attempt dating from the late 1970s was made by AAI of Baltimore under the auspices of the US Army Armament Research and Development Command (AARADCOM). AAI took the basic design of a 20mm experimental cannon devised by them and scaled it down to take existing 12.7 × 99mm ammunition. The demonstrator gun, nicknamed the Dover Devil, had the usual air-cooled barrel and was gas-operated. Its main innovation was a dual feed that could transfer feeding from one side to the other at the flick of a switch. This allowed instant selection of the type of ammunition to suit each fire mission, for instance swapping from, say, armour piercing to solid ball at will.

Despite weighing about half that of the M2 the Dover Devil did not find acceptance and faded away. But the overall design did find attractions elsewhere. In late 1983 a team led by Scot Sandy Cormack for Chartered Industries of Singapore (now Singapore Technologies Kinetics, or ST Kinetics) began design work on a 12.7mm machine gun generally similar to the Dover Devil. The new gun became known as the 50MG, displaying many of the overall features of the Dover Devil, including the dual feed, but with enough detail differences to make the 50MG a new design. For instance, 50MG construction is completely modular, having only five main assemblies. If any module goes wrong it can be rapidly

NSV-12.7	
Model	NSV-12.7
Calibre	12.7mm (0.50in)
Length	1,560mm (61.4in)
Weight	25kg (55.1lb)
Muzzle velocity	845m/s (2,772ft/sec)
Rate of fire	700–800rds/min
Feed	belt

The 50MG from Singapore, seen here on a light naval mounting.

replaced by a new module. This includes the barrel, replaceable within seconds. To extend the utility of the 50MG the 12.7mm SLAP (Saboted Light Armour Penetrator) armour-piercing round was developed locally.

The 50MG was put into production for the Singapore armed forces, but as far as is known there have been no other sales. With the Singapore armed forces the 50MG is employed in several roles, including on naval pintle mountings, although the usual land role is on a tripod or mounted on an armoured vehicle weapon station, alongside a 40mm automatic grenade launcher.

50MG	
Model	50MG
Calibre	12.7mm (0.50in)
Length	1,143mm (45in)
Weight	30kg (66.14lb)
Muzzle velocity	890m/s (2,920ft/sec)
Rate of fire	600rds/min
Feed	belt

20 More Lights

At the start of World War II the light machine gun was well established as the main infantry squad fire support weapon. Since that time its development and improvement has not ceased but has followed at least three avenues of progression. These have been the adoption of smaller calibres, the rise of the heavy barrel assault rifle, and the progress of the light machine gun itself. This chapter will concentrate on the light machine gun as a distinct entity.

JOHNSON

One light machine gun now often overlooked was the Johnson, although for its origins we have to return to the late 1930s. At that time Melvin Johnson, a lawyer from Boston who preferred designing small arms rather than following his trained profession, devised a recoil-operated semi-automatic rifle with some innovative features. The most important of these in the long term was the rotary bolt head, which had eight lugs that turned 20 degrees after firing before they could unlock and allow the bolt to recoil safely by blowback. Multi-lug locking is now almost universally applied, but it is often forgotten that it first appeared in its present form on the Johnson rifle.

Johnson, a Marine Corps Reserve officer, did his utmost to draw attention to his rifle but by the time it was ready the US Army had already selected the M1 Garand for series production. Attempts to promote the merits of the Johnson product created quite a political controversy for a while, but the Garand selection prevailed. The only Johnson rifle sales, apart from a few sporting guns, were to the Dutch East Indies; the bulk of them were taken over by the US Marines in early 1942 and retained only until Garands became available.

This preamble is provided only to demonstrate how unlucky a talented designer can be, in that Johnson's rifle simply appeared at the wrong time. The same thing happened with the Johnson light machine gun brought out in 1941 at about the same time as the rifle. It had even less chance of acceptance. The Browning Automatic Rifle was by then well entrenched and was not considered due for replacement, so Johnson's product once again went nowhere. Examples were manufactured alongside the rifles at the Johnson Automatics Company of Cranston, Rhode Island.

Although tested by the Marines the Johnson gun was rejected as being too flimsy and prone to jamming. However, in early 1942 and, at that time, being at the back of the queue when it came to new equipment issue, the US Marines Corps was

Johnson	
Model	Johnson
Calibre	7.62mm (0.30in)
Length	1.066mm (42in)
Weight	6.48kg (14.3lb)
Muzzle velocity	853m/s (2,800ft/sec)
Rate of fire	>900rds/min
Feed	20-round box

forced to accept part of the production batch of about 5,000, the rest going to US Army special forces. Both formations replaced them as soon as they could. The Johnson Model 1941 employed the same rotary bolt as the rifle and fed ammunition from a curved box on the left of the receiver, something that made the gun unbalanced. The magazine held twenty rounds, while, when fully loaded, a further five were inside the gun itself. Johnson also introduced a variable fire rate of from 300 to 900rds/min, controlled by altering the buffer spring tension.

Johnson brought out a slightly revised version of his gun in 1944, but it also got nowhere and he eventually became a technical consultant to a small arms development called Armalite. It seemed his machine gun was another destined to the recesses of small arms history but there was one final manifestation, although it seems that Johnson himself had nothing to do with it. During the late 1940s what appeared to be a copy of the Johnson Model 1944 was manufactured in Israel, chambered for 7.92 × 57mm ammunition. Known as the Dror, this derivative did not perform well, being prone to the ingress of dust and dirt, while the side-mounted magazine made handling awkward. The Dror was withdrawn and replaced after only a few years' service.

RPD

In parallel with German infantry planners, the concept of a lower powered rifle cartridge that could be shoulder-fired from light automatic weapons had long been recognized by Soviet ammunition designers. For various reasons, work on a 5.45mm round did not begin until 1939 and was then postponed when the Winter War with Finland started. It was not until 1943 that the project was revived, by that time with a 7.62 × 39mm intermediate cartridge to make maximum use of existing production tooling.

The final cartridge selected, the 7.62 × 39mm M1943, turned out to be one of the most successful and widely used cartridges ever devised, for, in time, it came to be the cartridge fired from the Kalashnikov AK-47 and AKM assault rifles, the most prolific infantry weapons ever produced. It was therefore logistically appropriate for the squad light machine gun to fire the same ammunition, so from 1944 onwards a series of trials continued until yet another design from the versatile Vasiliy Degtyarev won through. Mainly due to a period of clearing up after the war years, production of the Degtyarev gun, the 7.62mm RPD, did not commence until the early 1950s and continued (in the Soviet Union) until about 1960.

Although this example is an Israeli 7.92mm Dror, it is visually similar to the original Johnson light machine gun.

The 7.62mm RPD light machine gun with its bipod folded.

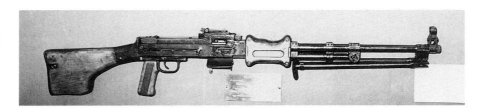

How many RPDs were manufactured has not been discovered but the numbers must have been large. It became the standard squad light machine gun throughout the Soviet armed forces and many Warsaw Pact forces. The RPD is belt-fed and gas-operated, the locking action involving lugs pushed into position by a wedge on top of the bolt carrier. Much of the rest of the mechanism was copied direct from the DP and fire remains fully automatic only. Bursts have to be limited as the barrel is fixed and soon overheats.100-round belts are carried in a drum clipped under the gun at the point of balance, preventing the belt from flapping about and snagging on anything nearby. One practical touch is that the butt contains a multi-section cleaning rod.

Throughout its relatively short production life at least five improvements were introduced, most of them relating to the gas-operation mechanism. The RPD was licence-produced in North Korea (Type 62) and may still be available from Norinco of China (Type 56-1). The RPD is still manufactured in Egypt as the 7.62mm Suez.

The RPD was eventually replaced by the RPK (*see* following chapter) but can still be encountered almost anywhere, particularly throughout Africa and South-East Asia. It remains a sound and practical squad automatic weapon.

STONER

Eugene M. Stoner (1922–97) was one of the small arms design giants of the post-1945 era. His main place in history is that he was the 'Father of the M16', the ubiquitous 5.56mm assault rifle exceeded in production terms only by the Kalashnikovs. The key to Stoner's success was the reinvention of the rotary bolt head locking system first featured on the recoil-operated Johnson guns but allied to gas operation.

The bulk of Stoner's design work related to assault rifles, in particular the series of rifles developed for the Armalite Corporation of Costa Mesa, California, the company's famous AR-15 becoming the M16. At one stage Stoner transferred his skills to the Colt's Patent Firearms Corporation and then the Cadillac Gage Corporation, where, among other projects, he began serious design work on a modular weapon family that could be modified to various configurations in the field as and when required. There were six configuration options available, all formed using allied groups of basic components, starting with an assault rifle and sub-machine gun, two forms of light machine gun (magazine or belt-fed), a medium machine gun for firing from a tripod, and a fixed gun for armoured vehicles.

Stoner produced the first designs in this family in 1962, chambered for 7.62 × 51mm ammunition. That was the Stoner 62. As it seemed very likely that a changeover to 5.56 × 45mm ammunition was imminent all further development work

RPD	
Model	RPD
Calibre	7.62mm (0.30in)
Length	1,041mm (41in)
Weight	7kg (15.44lb)
Muzzle velocity	734m/s (2,410ft/sec)
Rate of fire	700rds/min
Feed	100-round belt

The full array of the Stoner 63 7.62mm machine-gun family.

concentrated on that calibre, resulting in the Stoner 63.

Although it promised much, the Stoner 63 approach never did catch on. The US Marines tested the system, concentrating mainly on the assault rifle and light machine-gun models, and suggested some modifications, resulting in the 5.56mm Stoner 63A. A batch of belt-fed Stoner 63A light machine guns was procured for evalu-

ation by US Navy SEAL teams and used in combat in Vietnam, but their tenure of active service was relatively short. Attempts to manufacture the family in the Netherlands came to naught and the Stoner 63A faded from view.

However, Stoner had not done with machine guns. At one stage he formed an association with the ARES concern, designing a series of dedicated 5.56mm light machine guns that culminated in his final model, eventually taken over by the Knight's Armament Company of Vero Beach, Florida. His last model was a very attractive and practical gun weighing only 7.3kg (16.1lb) with a 200-round belt in a box under the gun, and with a choice of two barrel lengths, the shortest (397mm/15.5in) intended for the close-quarter combat role. For extreme portability the overall length can be reduced to just 660mm (25.7in) with the butt stock removed. Combat accessory rails are lavishly provided around the forward hand guard.

The latest Stoner gun has attracted great interest from special forces around the world, although to date none have been known to have been purchased in any quantity.

MINIMI

As will be outlined in the following chapter, light machine-gun development virtually ceased with the appearance of the heavy barrel squad fire support weapons based on assault rifles. At least one concern, FN of Belgium, thought otherwise.

The compact Stoner 5.56mm light machine gun, the last machine gun to bear the Stoner name, now marketed by Knight's Armament Company of Florida.

FN proved to be right, for no heavy barrel assault rifle can deliver the firepower possible from a dedicated belt-fed light machine gun.

Belgian development work on what was to become the 5.56mm Minimi light machine gun began during the early 1960s when coincidental investigations were being made into improving the efficiency of 5.56 × 45mm ammunition. This calibre was developed in the USA following studies relating to combat ranges and the dreadful-sounding wound ballistics. The studies confirmed that not only were nearly all combat engagements conducted at ranges under 400m (438yd) or so, but a small calibre high-velocity bullet could inflict lethal wounds at those ranges. There was therefore no need to retain the full calibre rounds such as 7.62mm, 7.92mm and 0.303 with their potential to deliver accurate fire to more than 1,000m (1,094yd). Smaller rounds could be shoulder-fired on fully automatic, while the number of rounds a soldier carried into action could be increased. Similar studies in the old Soviet Union resulted in a 5.45 × 39mm round.

Working against the contemporary grain, FN designers decided to develop a belt-fed squad fire support weapon in the new 5.56mm calibre. Work began under the aegis of Ernest Vervier, the designer responsible for the MAG, and was completed by Maurice Bourlet. An indication of the thorough development of the Minimi can be judged by the prototypes appearing in 1974, with production not starting until 1982. The amount of time spent testing or modifying during that period was prodigious but it paid dividends.

One result is that the Minimi is in a class of its own, with few competitors. In overall terms it is a mini MAG with a similar gas-operation system and trigger group. Locking is the now universal rotating bolt head but with a few FN innovations. The ammunition feed is unusual, for in addition to the 200-round belt feed from a clipped-on plastic container under the receiver there is also the facility to insert M16 pattern thirty-round box magazines without modification. Magazines can be inserted directly into an angled underside housing. A hot barrel can be replaced within

The Standard model of the FN Herstal 5.56mm Minimi light machine gun with its ammunition box installed.

This illustration clearly indicates the compact dimensions of the FN Herstal 5.56mm Minimi.

seconds. Firing stability and a steady fire rate can be enhanced by the addition of a hydraulic buffer; however, they are already so stable that demonstrations of the Minimi often involve it being fired from one hand like an oversize pistol.

There are three main Minimi models. The Standard has all the trimmings and a fixed butt stock, although the latter can be replaced by a collapsible stock if required. It was this Standard version that, with a few minor alterations, was adopted by the US Army and Marine Corps as their M249 Squad Automatic Weapon, or SAW. The M249 SAW is manufactured in the USA by FN Manufacturing Inc. of Columbia, South Carolina.

Then there is the Minimi Para model with a short barrel and the collapsible butt stock as standard. Some US units use their M249 SAWs with the short barrel.

The M240 also has a Special Purpose Weapon (SPW) variant devised in the USA, now also marketed by FN back in Belgium. The SPW is very much a US Special Forces 750rds/min 'get out of trouble quick' weapon with the accent on portability and reduced weight. The magazine feed option is omitted while there is provision to install combat accessories such as a forward pistol grip and various optical sights. The bipod is

The 'get out of trouble fast' version of the 5.56mm Minimi, the Special Purpose Weapon (SPW).

The Australian 5.56mm F89, the fully developed local variant of the Minimi with changes to suit local requirements.

usually left off the SPW. Weight is then reduced to 5.75kg (12.7lb) compared to 7.1kg (15.7lb) for the standard model.

The US armed forces have not been the only takers for the Minimi – it has been delivered to over thirty countries. Apart from production in the USA and Belgium, it has been licence-produced in Australia (at the Lithgow facility and known as the F89), Italy and Greece. The Combined Service Arsenals on Taiwan have produced a weapon almost identical to the Minimi, known as the 5.56mm Type 75. The South Korean 5.56mm Daewoo K3 also appears to have affiliations with the Minimi.

With all its many owners the Minimi has displayed a remarkable ability to withstand the roughest conditions and hard use. The US Army and Marines have a requirement expected to exceed 72,000, intending to keep their SAWs until at least 2012.

The Minimi will be around for a long time yet, with new customers constantly appearing, one of the latest (2002) being the British Army for troops serving in Afghanistan.

NEGEV

One of the few competitors to the Minimi is the 5.56mm Negev manufactured and marketed by Israel Military Industries (IMI) at its Ramat Hasharon facility. As with the Minimi, the Negev is a purpose-designed weapon but with its utility extending beyond the usual squad fire support function to vehicle, naval and helicopter mountings. It is one of the few weapons of its type

Minimi	
Model	Minimi
Calibre	5.56mm (0.22in)
Length	1,030mm (40.55in)
Weight	6.83kg (15lb)
Muzzle velocity	925m/s (3,035ft/sec)
Rate of fire	700–1,000rds/min
Feed	belt

The standard infantry form of the Israeli IMI 5.56mm Negev light machine gun.

that can launch rifle grenades from over its muzzle.

In operating terms the Negev differs little from other similar weapons, but it is constructed extremely well to withstand the conditions under which the Israel Defense Forces operate. Rapid and easy handling is paramount on the Negev, especially relating to ammunition feed. Fabric pouch belt containers for 150- or 200-round belts are clipped under the weapon, with the ability,

once all belts have been fired, to utilize M16 or Galil box magazines from the rest of the squad, although a magazine adaptor is required. There is also the option of a 380-round box.

The Negev usually has a bipod, although on the short-barrelled Negev-Commando variant it is usually left off. The Negev-Commando is very much an assault fire support weapon, having an angled forward grip. Its butt stock, as with the ordinary Negev model, is foldable to reduce the

The Negev-Commando, the assault version of the IMI 5.56mm Negev light machine gun intended for hand-held deployments only.

Negev	
Model	Negev
Calibre	5.56mm (0.22in)
Length	1,020mm (40.15in)
Weight	7.2kg (15.9lb)
Muzzle velocity	850m/s (2,789ft/sec)
Rate of fire	650–800rds/min
Feed	belt

overall length. The Negev-Commando weighs 6.95kg (15.3lb) as opposed to 7.6kg (16.8lb) for the usual version, and its overall length can be reduced to just 680mm (26.5in).

The Israel Defense Forces utilize the Negev as their standard infantry squad fire support weapon although, as indicated above, it has also found numerous other roles to play.

ULTIMAX

The Singapore Technologies Kinetics 5.56mm Ultimax 100 is one automatic weapon that somehow manages to straddle the divide between automatic rifles and light machine guns. Fully loaded with a 100-round drum and the bipod installed, the Ultimax 100 weighs only 6.8kg (15lb), making it only slightly heavier than many assault rifles. Yet the quick-change barrel can

The 5.56mm Ultimax from Singapore, one of the lightest machine guns in its class.

sustain 500 rounds of fully automatic fire (an unlikely probability during almost any firefight) without heat damage.

The Ultimax 100 was developed by a team that included ex-Armalite director James Sullivan, so it is no surprise that the operating mechanism has much in common with that of the M16 rifle. Work on the Ultimax started in 1978, with the first prototypes ready by mid-1979 and the first production models appearing in 1982. That was the Ultimax Mark 2 with a fixed barrel. The Mark 3 has a quick-change barrel.

The low weight of the Ultimax 100 is combined with extremely low recoil, even during bursts. This combination makes it an ideal weapon for the smaller-statured military populations of parts of South-East Asia. The low recoil is produced mainly by an extremely long recoil spring arranged around a guide rod in such a manner that the usual buffer or recoil cylinder arrangements are not necessary. The fully automatic-only cyclic fire rate is also low, from 500 to 540rds/min, making gun control that much easier. All these features combine to make the Ultimax 100 an ideal 'assault' weapon, an asset further assisted by the provision of a forward hand-grip and the ability to remove the butt stock. The gun can even be fired effectively from the shoulder in the same manner as a rifle.

The 100-round plastic drums have a clear rear face to allow the gunner to see easily how many rounds remain to be fired. If no drums are available M16 pattern magazines can be used instead.

Overall, manufacturing the Ultimax 100 is straightforward and relatively low-cost, with even the barrels remaining unchromed.

One of the most unusual aspects of the Ultimax 100 is that it can accommodate a bayonet. Another unusual accessory is a muzzle-attached sound suppressor developed in the Philippines, although here the intention is not to make the gun soundless but to conceal the firing signature (both noise and flash) so that a firing position is more difficult to detect.

Apart from sales to the local defence forces, Ultimax 100 sales have been made to nations such as Honduras, the Philippines and Zimbabwe. One mystery still remaining to be cleared up is how numbers of Ultimax 100s managed to appear in action during the upheavals in the Balkans in the 1990s. It seems that Croatia, at least, was an Ultimax 100 owner. The Ultimax 100 Mark 3 is still being marketed.

Ultimax 100	
Model	Ultimax 100
Calibre	5.56mm (0.22in)
Length	1,030mm (40.55in)
Weight	4.7kg (10.36lb) unloaded
Muzzle velocity	890m/s (2,920ft/sec)
Rate of fire	500–540rds/min
Feed	100-round drum

H&K AGAIN

During 2001 it was announced that Heckler & Koch had designed a 5.56mm light machine gun intended to counter the Belgian Minimi's market domination. Even though the Minimi has been sold to over thirty countries, H&K is aware that other countries are learning the limitations of heavy barrelled assault-rifle fire support weapons (*see* following Chapter), and are thinking of adopting some form of dedicated light machine gun in their place. One such nation, for example, is the UK, which adopted Minimis for operations in Afghanistan (although on a temporary expedient basis).

H&K therefore developed its 5.56mm MG43. Relatively little has been released regarding this promising design, although two things are known. One is that it successfully completed extensive trials under desert conditions. The second is that it has an extremely powerful pawl feeding mechanism capable of lifting and reliably loading belts many hundreds of rounds long. Another advanced feature is the provision of a number of safety systems to make the gun as safe as conceivably possible. Firing is automatic only, there is a rapid barrel-change system, and the gun is stated to be able to fire bursts in the 'sustained-fire mode'. Gun weight is only 6.4kg (14.1lb).

A bipod is standard, as is a side-folding butt stock. The fire controls are so arranged that the gun can be fired even with the stock folded. Generous lengths of MIL-STD-1913 Picatinny rail are provided for mounting various types of sighting system.

With the MG43 hardly out of the prototype stage there is little more to be said of it, other than it seems to be a very promising design.

Perhaps an indication of things to come, the Heckler & Koch 5.56mm MG43.

21 Automatic Rifles

It seems safe to state that the first of a whole string of automatic rifles was the Browning Automatic Rifle (*see* Chapter 11). For its time the BAR was an extremely effective weapon, but one of its main shortcomings was the inability to deliver anything other than short bursts, with frequent intervals between them. The alternative was an overheated barrel, which, if suffered long enough, could be irreparably damaged or impose other malfunctions. Matters were not helped by the employment of a full-power rifle cartridge with its attendant recoil forces and limited magazine capacity.

The BAR did have one important place in small arms history in that it fully demonstrated the utility of a squad fire support weapon that could be issued on a wide scale to provide the all-important 'base of fire' so important to any infantry operation. For a long time the light machine gun appeared to be the main provider of the required firepower, but during the 1950s the BAR concept was revived once again.

By then the old BARs were fading away due to age and the advent of the assault rifle. However, even with the introduction of the automatic assault rifle, something was still needed to provide a firepower base. A move began to take the assault rifle of the time and provide it with a heavier barrel and a bipod. This approach offered the advantages of commonality between weapon types and ammunition calibres within a squad, plus the ability for the same magazines to be used on both weapons.

Unfortunately, this approach has been considered by many observers to be faulty. The first indications why emerged when, thanks to political and military attitudes of the day, the US Army decided to retain a full-power rifle cartridge and virtually impose it on other NATO countries instead of considering the combat and other attractions of the intermediate power, small calibres. During 1957, the US Army adopted the M14 rifle, an enhanced M1 Garand, firing the 7.62 × 51mm cartridge. As the old 0.30-06 BAR could not fire the same cartridge, a squad fire support weapon was needed so the BAR concept was adapted by fitting a fixed heavy barrel, revised all-in-line layout and bipod on to the M14A1.

To say the M14A1 was successful is less than honest. Even the M14 had to be fired on semi-automatic only to provide anything approaching accuracy, due to the significant recoil forces produced. Despite all its provisions, the M14A1 proved to be equally inaccurate, jumping about on firing at the full cyclic rate of 750rds/min. In addition, the twenty-round M14 magazine limited the amount of firepower that could be delivered. If sustained firing did arise, the barrel soon got too hot for further use. US soldiers came to view the M14A1 with distaste, but it survived in service for years until its drawbacks indicated what to avoid along the way ahead. It therefore laid the foundations for the adoption of the M249 SAW (*see* previous chapter). However, there were many convoluted diversions on the road to the M249, too many to cover within these pages.

A similar Canadian conversion of the Belgian 7.62mm FN FAL, the C2, was equally unsuccessful.

An indication of how the heavy-barrel concept originally developed, the Canadian 7.62mm FN FAL C2 without a magazine installed.

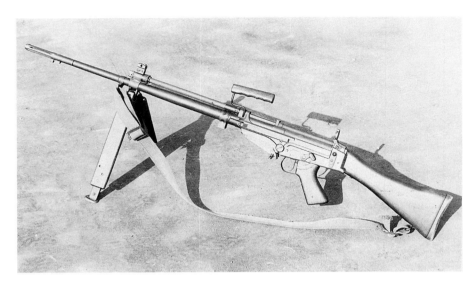

SMALL CALIBRES

With acceptance of the 7.62mm NATO round and the small calibre 5.56 or 5.45mm cartridges, it became time for another sequence of heavy-barrelled assault rifles. The same advantages were promised – logistic, financial and maintenance being to the fore – but the end results for the soldier in the field have too often been less than expected.

Several examples of this can be quoted. One comes from what is now Russia where the adoption of the 5.45mm AK-74 rifle meant that the 7.62mm RPD could no longer remain as a front-line squad fire support weapon. Its place was taken by the 5.45mm RPK-74, a longer, heavier-barrelled version of the AK-74 assault rifle. A bipod is added and the foldable butt stock revised in outline. Apart from the usual AK-74 thirty-round box magazines, forty or forty-five-round magazines are available.

The problem remains that the barrel is fixed and soon overheats, as with all other similar designs. Soldiers are trained to fire the RPK-74 in short bursts only, limiting its tactical utility and potential firepower. This basic shortcoming simply has

to be accepted as there is no way around it. It also has to be said that the RPK-74 is now widely employed, not only in what is now the Russian Federation but throughout the former Warsaw Pact nations. The RPK-74 has also been licence-produced in Bulgaria, China and Romania. The RPK-74M is an improved version featuring plastic furniture in place of the original wood. An export model of the latter is chambered for 5.56mm ammunition.

In short and in the vernacular, when push comes to shove the heavy-barrel assault rifle cannot hack it. The main shortcomings can be overcome by the adoption of a belt feed and/or some type of barrel change, creating in effect a dedicated light machine gun. This is at last being appreciated by many who have invested in the heavy barrel approach, but assault rifle 'families' are still appearing, consisting usually of an assault rifle, carbine, marksman model and a heavy-barrel squad fire support weapon. There is no need to go into every instance of this, but a short list of current 'host' assault rifles with associated heavy-barrel variants is provided here.

In this list, mention is made of only one M16 derivative squad weapon, but over the years there

Austria	5.56mm AUG
Canada	Diemaco 5.56mm C7
China	5.56mm Type 97
	5.8mm Type 95
Czech Republic	5.56mm CZ 2000
Germany	H&K 5.56mm HK11
	H&K 5.56mm G36
India	5.56mm INSAS
Israel	5.56mm Galil
Italy	Beretta 5.56mm AS70/90
Poland	5.56mm Beryl mod.96
Singapore	5.56mm SAR 21
UK	5.56mm SA-80 (L86)
USA	5.56mm Colt M16A2

G36

Model	G36
Calibre	5.56mm (0.22in)
Length	990mm (39in)
Weight	3.98kg (8.77lb)
Muzzle velocity	920m/s (3,018ft/sec)
Rate of fire	750rds/min
Feed	30-round box

L86A1

Model	L86A1
Calibre	5.56in (0.22in)
Length	900mm (35.4in)
Weight	7.28kg (16lb)
Muzzle velocity	970m/s (3,182ft/sec)
Rate of fire	610–775rds/min
Feed	30-round box

have been many. Indeed, the list is not comprehensive for many trials models from many countries have emerged over the years, usually destined to disappear for one reason or another.

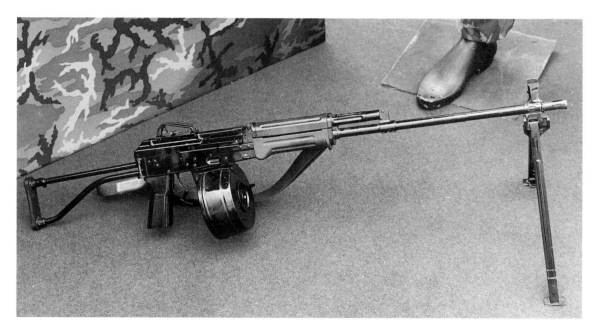

The Czech CZ 2000 5.45mm light machine gun, actually a CZ 2000 assault rifle with an extended heavy barrel.

The 5.56mm Colt Automatic rifle, basically a much modified M16 assault rifle with a ninety-round magazine in addition to a heavy barrel.

The Indian 5.56mm INSAS light machine gun, the squad light-support version of the INSAS assault rifle.

Showing its close affiliations with the AK-47/AKM assault rifles, the Russian 7.62mm RPK.

The light squad fire support version of the Heckler & Koch 5.56mm G36 rifle.

22 Driven

Exponents of the machine gun have long been giving consideration to how rapid their rate of fire should be. During World War II fire rates of up to 1,300rds/min were being delivered from guns such as the MG42. Many saw no real tactical reason to produce such rates for land service as they often just wasted ammunition (targets on the receiving end usually thought otherwise). But for air warfare there was a different case to be answered. Aircraft targets can be small and fleeting, so the time periods during which effective fire can be produced are limited to fractions of a second.

There are practical limits to the fire rates at which recoil or gas-operated weapons can function. At extreme firing rates the mechanical components involved will be operating at the critical limits of their mechanical strength, usually only just below a critical level. In the past the desired firepower for aircraft has been by multiple gun installations, from four to eight being the norm, although some aircraft had more. With the arrival of the jet age, aircraft speeds became such that even massed cannon installations had limitations.

The search for a new method of producing automatic fire was already in progress when World War II ended. By then, consideration was already being given to externally powered machine guns. The attractions were obvious. By providing an external power source, limitations imposed by the power of the ammunition to drive the load/fire/extraction/reload processes could be overcome. Further limitations imposed by ammunition malfunctions, always a primary source of machine-gun

stoppages, could be surmounted by driving dud rounds out of the gun. By varying the speed of the power source, firing rates could be altered at will and under positive control.

Not forgetting that manual drive is an external power, its origins go back to the period when manually operated guns were the rule, one prime example being the Gatling Gun. As early as 1893 an electric motor had been harnessed to a Gatling Gun for trials, with the result that the cyclic rate reached 3,000rds/min. Nothing came of that project for there was then no application for such a contrivance. The same no doubt happened to a 1920s experiment in Turkey when an intrepid local designer used a small petrol engine to drive a gun – the result can be found in the recesses of the Askeri Müzesi in Istanbul.

MINIGUN

In 1945 General Electric was asked to develop some form of rapid-firing aircraft gun and decided upon a powered Gatling Gun. Experiments duplicating the Gatling 1893 experiment (with a 0.45in Model 1883 gun) demonstrated cyclic rates of about 5,800rds/min. The result was *Project Vulcan*, a programme to develop a 20mm Gatling-pattern cannon that became the M61 Vulcan. In almost all respects the method of operation was exactly the same as the Gatling original, the only real difference being the electric drive resulting in a cyclic rate of 6,000rds/min. The M61 was installed in many types of fighter aircraft and went on to have air defence gun applications as well.

US Air Force personnel preparing an SUU-11/A 7.62mm Minigun pod on an AC-47 'Puff the Magic Dragon'.

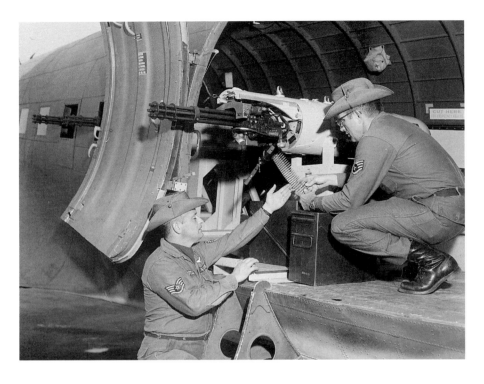

A 7.62 × 51mm Gatling offshoot from *Project Vulcan* began in 1960 and became the M134 (Army) or GAU-2B/A (Air Force) Minigun. Once again, General Electric was involved, funded by the US Air Force. The gun first went into action over Vietnam in 1964, the intention usually being to deliver suppressive fire from helicopters or aircraft such as the AC-47 'Puff the Magic Dragon'. By circling a target area the combined firepower of three or four Miniguns could be concentrated on one point. As each gun could fire extended bursts at 6,000rds/min (that is 100 rounds each second) and sometimes higher, with extended bursts lasting many seconds, the devastating firepower of such installations can be appreciated. Miniguns were also carried as side-firing guns by UH-1 series helicopters to clear landing areas or eliminate sources of enemy fire, often breaking up Vietcong attacks before they could even begin.

The 7.62mm Minigun, operating in exactly the same manner as the original Gatling Gun, relies on a 24–28-volt source of electrical power. That source is processed to vary the firing rate as required and to speed the transport of long and heavy metal-link ammunition belts all the way from the large magazines stowed somewhere close to the gun and into the gun. This is in addition to driving the six barrels for the loading, chambering, firing, extracting and reloading cycles. Many Minigun installations were contained within pods to simplify matters and keep them compact.

With the end of the Vietnam campaign interest in the Minigun began to wane. Many were passed to nations such as Israel, Australia and the UK (RAF), although US holdings of the Minigun were never allowed to vanish completely, for the gun reappeared as the armament of AC-130 gunships during the Afghanistan operations of 2002. By then, much had happened and thereby hangs a little bit of history.

While the M134 Minigun itself might have been satisfactory, the same could not be said of its peripheral bits and pieces. In fact, the gun had gained something of a reputation for being complicated and troublesome. In addition, General Electric, eventually part of General Dynamics Armament Systems, withdrew Minigun production availability and after-sales support.

All this became highlighted when Mike Dillon of Scottsdale, Arizona, obtained a second-hand batch of Miniguns to use as an engineering exercise. He found several things he did not like. Firstly, he did away with the several heavy, bulky and unreliable power supply and control units. Thanks to modern technology, they were replaced by a single small unit on the gun, just in front of the spade grips and a fire control unit was also added. This alone did much to make the gun more reliable and compact. The magazine hoppers became another subject of attention. Not only were they complicated items, they were also slow to reload. They were much simplified, introducing added details such as a funnel-shaped chute that realigns any out-of-line cartridges in the belt.

One major source of the original troubles was the point where cartridges are removed from their belt links just prior to loading into the gun. This

M134 Minigun	
Model	M134 Minigun
Calibre	7.62mm (0.30in)
Length	801.6mm (31.56in)
Weight	16.3kg (35.9lb)
Muzzle velocity	869m/s (2,851ft/sec)
Rate of fire	>6,000rds/min
Feed	belt

can be a trouble-prone operation on any machine gun, but on the Minigun any de-linking jam when airborne resulted in having to virtually strip down that area of the gun and spend several minutes clearing the problem – all in an open helicopter hatch while being shot at. Ingenious re-engineering by Mike Dillon and his Dillon Aerospace team removed that problem to the extent that his de-linking unit has been retrofitted to many original Miniguns. Several other gun mechanism access points were rendered more user-friendly. The fire rate became fixed at 3,000rds/min, quite adequate for any fire mission while

Firing 3,000rds/min from a Dillon 7.62mm Minigun from the side of a Huey helicopter.

A 0.50/12.7mm GAU-19/A three-barrelled machine gun mounted on a UAE HMMWV.

Firing a 0.50/12.7mm GAU-19/A machine gun from a much-modified 'Desert' Land Rover.

reducing component stresses and improving overall reliability. Dillon also introduced numerous other design details, some to the bolt configuration to improve reliability. The result is an ultra-reliable and smoothly functioning Minigun, now in production and with detail development continuing (such as with a gun mounting battery pack). As Mike Dillon has stated, 'The M134 and the Dillon gun may look alike but the only thing they have in common is that both were made in America.'

As before, the main applications are seen as helicopter installations. One ground-based project involves an ordinary pick-up truck to be added to a VIP or critical supply escort column. It may look like an inoffensive vehicle, but at any sign of ambush or trouble the Dillon Minigun pops up through the roof to make those concerned change their minds.

OTHERS

The General Electric-powered Gatling approach extended to two other calibres in our sphere of interest. One is 0.50/12.7mm. The model is the GECAL 50 or GAU-19/A, firing standard 12.7 × 99mm ammunition and dating from 1983. This operates in exactly the same way as the Minigun, although only three barrels are involved – prototypes had six. This time two fixed fire rates are available, 1,000 or 2,000rds/min.

The GAU-19/A has found naval and ground applications, such as arming HMMWV high mobility vehicles for nations such as the United Arab Emirates. The same cannot be said of another General Electric project, this time a 5.56mm model officially known as the Microgun but usually named the Six Pack from the number of barrels.

Exactly what tactical role the Six Pack was supposed to fulfil was never explained. It could fire at practical rates of more than 4,000rds/min, but its range and on-target performance were limited to ranges much shorter than its 7.62mm

Minigun counterpart, too short for tactical comfort. Only prototypes were made and the Six Pack project was eventually dropped. The US Army did test the gun under the designation XM214, including on light tripods with battery packs nearby, but the programme went no further.

CHAINS

The Minigun and its ilk are not the only externally driven machine guns. Also available are the single-barrelled Chain Guns, where an electrical motor provides the power and all internal actions are driven and timed by an internal industrial-strength chain loop in a 'race track' configuration

A demonstration example of a 7.62mm EX-34 Chain Gun.

around four sprockets, one providing the drive. As the chain is driven around, a slider on a master link moves the bolt carrier backwards and forwards. The gun therefore does not rely on power from the ammunition to operate and all stages of machine-gun operation can be precisely timed and controlled.

The resultant fire rates are much lower than the electrically driven Gatlings can produce, but that matters little as they are quite adequate for ground combat. The so-called EX-34 Chain Gun produced in 7.62mm is limited to about 520–580 rds/min. The main application is as a coaxial gun for armoured vehicles, although helicopter installations remain available. Other models in the Chain Gun series have calibres up to 30mm, known collectively as the Bushmaster series.

The 7.62mm EX-34 was originally a product of the old Hughes Tool Company of Mesa, Arizona. After a series of corporate takeovers it is now the responsibility of Allied Techsystems (ATK). It remains available with two barrel lengths to suit the type of installation, spent cases being ejected forwards and with no fumes coming into the host vehicle due to the sealed receiver.

The promise of the 7.62mm Chain Gun has yet to materialize. It was selected for coaxial

mountings in British Army Warrior IFVs (as the L94A1), the only known EX-34 success to date. Those guns were licence-manufactured in the UK, the initial contract calling for 606.

Another ATK Chain Gun is in the offing, chambered once again for 12.7 × 99mm ammunition. Development commenced in August 2000. At the time of writing only test hardware had been produced, and the first two fully firing prototypes were not anticipated much before 2003. The gun is a scaled-down version of the Bushmaster 30mm MK44 cannon so is colloquially known as the 0.50 Baby Bushmaster. That means it has a dual belt feed system allowing the choice of two ammunition natures to suit the fire mission involved.

The anticipated rate of fire will be from 400 to 500rds/min, the electronic control system being pre-programmed for single shot, five, ten, or twenty rounds or unlimited bursts. One claimed advantage of the Baby Bushmaster is that a typical installation will weigh less than for a Browning M2. Thanks to the usual Chain Gun requirement for a 24–28-volt power supply, its main market is anticipated as armoured-vehicle applications, either as a coaxial gun or on an overhead weapon station. Some type of one-man turret installation is another possibility.

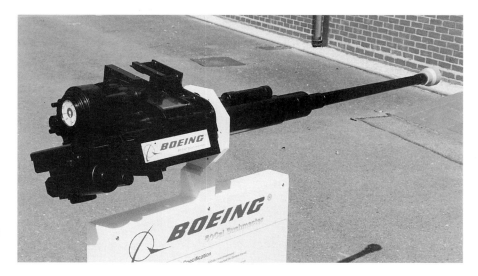

Latest in the chain-driven line, the 0.50/12.7mm Baby Bushmaster, now no longer a Boeing product but one from Allied Techsystems (ATK).

Finale

As stated at the beginning of this book, these pages cannot mention every type of machine gun manufactured or proposed, but the main milestones in machine-gun development have been covered. That development is still far from over. New models and types are constantly appearing, each with some technological innovation or operating novelty. Few basic changes can be anticipated for either recoil or gas-operated mechanisms, although it seems that externally powered gun development has yet to be exhausted.

Several completely new aspects of machine-gun technology can be anticipated, although they all appear to be a long way off. Something might yet be made of the now discarded technologies of the so-called 'Trounds' and their 'lockless' firing systems. The ammunition types in this latter category consist of projectiles set into a block of propellant inside a stout plastic case in such a manner that the case acts as its own breech block. There is therefore no need for case extraction or even bolts. The few lockless guns that reached the hardware stage fed their triangular cross-section Trounds from a hopper into a rotating drum assembly that simply holds the Tround when it is aligned with the barrel for firing. Fire rates of 2,000rds/min were achieved with demonstrator guns devised by the old Hughes Tool Company.

For many reasons the lockless gun concept got so far and no further. Yet it remains one of the paths that future development might follow. A related alternative is cased telescopic ammunition (CTA), with the projectile set into the propellant. This time a breech, probably rotating, provides

locking at the instant of firing. CTA rounds can be shorter (or more powerful for a given size) and handling is simplified considerably since the propellant block could be square or any other cross section. The CTA approach was adopted by Heckler & Koch for its 4.73 × 33mm round designed for the Heckler & Koch G11 assault rifle. That programme was terminated purely for national economic reasons in the aftermath of the collapse of the Berlin Wall but the technology survives, ready to be resurrected.

The same might be said regarding liquid propellants. The logistic, ballistic and handling merits of squirting the required volume of liquid propellant into a chamber at the instant of firing are self-evident to the extent that enormous sums of money have been spent attempting to achieve such a goal. To date, liquid propellants have emerged as a non-starter, with too many technical challenges still to be met. Yet one day solutions may be found.

Perhaps more imminent is the Metal Storm approach. Metal Storm is the result of a revolutionary approach to weapons operation by an Australian, Mike O'Dwyer. His approach to producing high fire volumes is to combine electronics with a novel form of propellant ignition. As a simplified outline, bullets are packed nose to tail inside a barrel with the required amount of propellant between each bullet. Starting from the front of the barrel, the first batch of propellant is ignited under electronic control. The resultant gas expansion not only drives the front bullet out of the barrel but acts against the next bullet, creating a seal that prevents detonation of the second load.

That second propellant load can then be ignited under electronic control, and so on. Once the barrel is empty it is replaced by a fresh factory-loaded item, either manually or mechanically, in exactly the same manner as existing ammunition feeds.

That is only a very broad outline of the Metal Storm system. Early test devices had massed barrels, set in a frame, each barrel holding ten 9mm bullets. Firing off the entire frame at one go produced bullet deliveries at a theoretical rate of 1,000,000rds/min. That remarkable output disguised the fact that, being electronically controlled, it is equally possible to fire off single shots or controlled rate bursts from single or multiple barrels, as required.

The Metal Storm approach is still in its infancy and could yet come to grief. Interest, both corporate and military, is growing as more and more possibilities emerge. One obstacle still to be overcome is the image of a system producing 1,000,000rds/min. That configuration was, after all, only a modern equivalent of the organ gun. Which is where we came in.

Index